Managing
Christian
Schools

Managing Christian Schools

A Handbook for Administrators, Teachers, and Board Members

Philip Elve

CSI PUBLICATIONS
Christian Schools International
School Relations Department
Grand Rapids, Michigan 49508

Christian Schools International
3350 East Paris Avenue, SE
P.O. Box 8709
Grand Rapids, Michigan 49508

IN CANADA:
P.O. Box 39
Norwich, Ontario N0J 1P0

ISBN: 0-87463-119-X

I gratefully acknowledge the help of Kenneth Swets and Dorothy Uiterdyk in editing and typing the manuscript.

Contents

Preface

This handbook began with the idea that Christian-school administration should be better understood by all those actively involved in managing Christian schools.

The board of directors of Christian Schools International (CSI) had expressed concern about what seemed to them to be a high rate of turnover among Christian-school administrators. The board asked their staff to conduct a study to determine what factors affected this turnover. The study, "Administrative Personnel Changes in CSI Member Christian Schools," was completed by the staff in 1980.

From this study, the board concluded that Christian Schools International must move to create a better understanding of Christian-school management techniques. One of its goals was to create a better understanding of the roles of Christian-school board members, teachers, and administrators.

This handbook, although emphasizing the administrator's responsibilities, also has much to say to teachers and board members. The aim of this publication is to provide better insights into the critical factors which influence the smooth operation and quality of a Christian school.

Each chapter addresses a critical aspect of Christian-school management. Written in a manner which will al-

low its use as an in-service tool for staff members and
board members, this handbook also prescribes programs
and procedures which school managers can use to improve their Christian school. Our hope is that it indeed
will be used to that end.

Philip Elve, Ph.D.

1

The Administrator

It hardly needs to be said that anyone who seeks to be a school principal ought to know what life will be like in the front office. Yet some who enter the profession are incredibly naive as to what school administration is all about. A few have an image in their minds of sitting comfortably in an office, serving as the "great white father." Others act as if they have just been given a large grab bag filled with goodies. They can hardly wait to see what is inside. What they will find is a mixed bag indeed. When things are going well, school administration can be a most satisfying responsibility. However, that grab bag may contain a mousetrap or two. When one reaches in, the result can be painful indeed.

Profile of a Good Administrator

In 1980 Philip Elve and Kenneth Swets of the Christian Schools International staff did a study entitled "Administrative Personnel Changes in CSI Member Schools." The study found that within the last three years 55 percent of all the administrators who responded to the questionnaire had considered leaving administration. They cited various reasons:

It appears that the time commitment involved in Christian school administration is viewed as the primary negative factor in remaining in the position. No doubt this situation is aggravated by the fact that many Christian-school administrators must also teach. Teaching preparations, administrative responsibilities, and meetings apparently create an unusual burden on some administrators and, consequently, on their families. Add to this the concern for salary, which is often only slightly above that of a teacher, and one can readily begin to understand why administrators sometimes decide to return to the classroom, or to a different position outside education.

One should not conclude from these findings that Christian-school administration is a wholly distasteful experience. On the contrary, positive responses to the questionnaire outnumbered negative responses almost two to one. Those who had the most positive attitude toward their work were those who enjoyed working with staff members and students.

The conclusion one reaches in reviewing this and similar studies is that those school administrators who really like working with people fare much better than those who do not. Those who lead by involving others in the decision-making process fare better than those who make decisions on their own. Those who view themselves as a colleague of the staff fare better than do those who view themselves as the boss. Those who consider themselves as serving the staff and students fare better than do those who regard the staff as serving them. The "givers" in administration are really the "receivers."

In addition to a desire to serve others, those who enter administration should have a talent for management and the ability to get others to work together for the common good. They should also acquire expertise in a number of areas. In a recent study experienced administrators listed those areas in which training is most important: school management, curriculum and program development, supervision of instruction, laws affecting the educational system, finance and budgeting, personnel administration, leadership, human relations, community relations, child development, psychology of learning, and counseling and guidance.

In view of the many facets of the job, it is no wonder that some administrators are overwhelmed by its pressures and demands; but many also report that they experience much satisfaction, a certain amount of prestige, and often self-fulfillment in their role. Most administrators achieve their goal of influencing educational decisions and planning. Many enjoy the leadership role and believe that they have the skills which will help them succeed in it. Many like the sense of control and the feeling of being in charge; to some, status is important. The higher salaries that school administration usually offers are no doubt an additional incentive for some, although the higher salaries earned by administrators are not all that impressive when one considers the length of the administrator's workday, workweek, and school year in comparison with that of the teacher.

One drawback for Christian-school administrators is the almost complete lack of opportunity for advancement. The most that Christian-school administrators can hope for is to move to a larger school. Few Christian-school systems have a superintendency or some other administrative position which carries responsibility over a number of schools. Many Christian-school administrators have, in fact, acquired advanced degrees only to find that they are educationally overqualified for the principalship and that there is no higher professional outlet for themselves within Christian schools. In these situations one can receive satisfaction from professional improvement and accomplishments rather than from advancement in position.

That a good teacher will automatically make a good administrator is a common misconception. Of course, being a good teacher helps, but being an administrator is really an entirely different profession, and good teachers do not necessarily make the best administrators. To be sure, there are certain qualities that good teachers and good administrators have in common, not the least of which is the ability to motivate others. That elusive thing called leadership is definitely helpful for both teacher and administrator; beyond a doubt it is an essential quality for an administrator.

The administrator also needs some other qualities which, while helpful to teachers, are essential for a supervisory position. For example, he or she must know how to make decisions—fast. This may conjure up the image of a judge on the bench with a stream of patrons seeking wisdom like that of Solomon. But this picture is erroneous, for the era of handing down decisions from on high has expired. The authority of the school administrator is no longer absolute. Such a change is for the better, but nonetheless it is a change some administrators regret. Today's administrator must be oriented to the new process of decision-making. It may be difficult for an administrator to recall even a few decisions which he or she has made exclusively within the last few months, but he or she surely can point to decisions which he or she has affected in one way or another.

The decision-making process is not without its frustrations. In a survey of some forty high-school administrators it was found that resolving conflicts is the greatest drain on their time. Tied in with this is the fact that too many people become too involved in the process. Yes, making an acceptable decision in school life today can be much more complicated than in the past. The same can be said for problem-solving because the problems administrators face today unfortunately can be far more complicated than those of the past. There was a day when a teacher's class schedule was merely handed out by the administrator. Today the professional teacher wants at least to be consulted, and the parent and even the student feel they should have something to say concerning those problems which affect them.

In spite of this network of involvement, the administrator is still considered to be the authority figure in the school. When things go wrong, the question, "Why doesn't the principal do something about it?" is heard in the teachers' lounge and parents' living rooms. He or she is, in effect, an authority figure without authority; or at least the authority is very much limited. Not overstepping what are perceived to be the bounds of the administrator's authority is a delicate balance, one which repeatedly places the administrator in a precarious position. The role of authority figure is not very comfortable for many administrators.

People who become angry with the school or someone on its staff will sooner or later take aim at the administrator. Students may take out their anger on the administrator's home or car. Parents may take out their frustrations by complaining to the school board. The school board will eventually get around to blaming their woes on the administrator: After all, "You wanted to run things. So run them right!" The CSI study previously cited reflected this aspect of the administrator's role:

> It also appears that the high incidence of difficulties in the human relations aspect of the job adds to a disillusionment which may be the 'last straw' precipitating a decision to leave. Many administrators apparently view the parents, staff, and board members as not always understanding the pressures associated with administrative jobs.

In spite of these difficulties the study also revealed that the majority of Christian-school administrators are happy in their work and regard it as an opportunity to be of real service and to affect others for good. A sound word of advice for administrators (and for anyone whose work involves serving other people) is not to expect too much in terms of praise and appreciation. It should be sufficient for one to know he or she is serving others to the best of his or her ability, that he or she is contributing to the welfare of others, that he or she is serving the Lord and His kingdom well, and that, for all those efforts, he or she receives a reasonably good livelihood for self and family.

Challenges Facing Today's Administrators

School administration is a challenge which has many faces. It not only has the dimensions of almost every administrative position in industry, but it also has the added dimension of dealing with people of all ages and the added challenge of applying the very complicated science of teaching. Often, in addition to the management aspects of the job, the administrator is expected to be an expert in child development, learning readiness, various learning styles, and effective teaching methods. No administrator can be an expert in every teaching area but every administrator should be knowledgeable in the teaching and learning processes. The administrator must get teachers to extend themselves, to go beyond what they think they can do, to try new ideas, to be stimulating for students, to show understanding, and to be content in a task which can be discouraging and trying at times.

The administrator gives guidance to the faculty and gets to know their strengths, weaknesses, style, and idiosyncrasies. The administrator motivates by compliments, support, and counsel. In all this he or she must become a skilled observer, an accurate evaluator, and a sympathetic adviser.

The administrator is always on the trail of ways to improve teaching for the child's sake. This means not only selecting the best people for the job, but also providing in-service training so teachers can continue to improve in carrying out their task.

There must be a bit of the lawyer in a good school administrator, for today we live within the web of school and civil law. The administrator must know what the government requires of the school, when the government is exceeding its authority, when the civil rights of staff members and students are being endangered.

A large array of voluntary associations, committees, and church bodies looks to the administrator for leadership. Wherever he or she appears in these arenas, he or she represents the school, Christian education, and self, and this gives the administrator a special responsibility. Not only will a high expectation of performance be placed upon him or her, but he or she will be considered as a reflection of what a Christian school is—and of what a Christian is.

School curriculum is a complicated field in and of itself. Some educators carve a career solely out of curriculum development, and then usually in only one or two subject areas. Yet in most Christian schools the administrator is conceived to be the leader in curriculum development. The principal needs to weigh each curriculum idea and suggestion in order to help the staff determine its worthiness and usefulness in the school. He or she needs the advice of those experts in each subject area, but this will not relieve him or her of the leadership and decision-making role in matters concerning curriculum.

No doubt the two most crucial areas of an administrator's expertise concern leadership in the spiritual dimensions of the school and in the area of human relationships. The Christian school is established for a specific purpose. Parents give their money and send their children to the Christian school because they want their children to have a God-centered education. They entrust the principal and the staff with the task of providing the child with a biblical view of the world and of life. The administrator is charged by the school board and the parents to see that the teaching in and the climate of the school conform to the spiritual values of the parents. Fulfillment of the main purpose of the Christian school depends to a great extent on the spiritual leadership of the administrator. The staff will look to him or her for the necessary spiritual leadership which places Christ's stamp upon the school, its teachings, and its students.

Human relationships also are an important aspect of successful school administration. Where people work together in any venture, there will be conflicting ideas, unwanted restraints, and imposition of special interests. The administrator must have the skill and the personal attributes to moderate any influences which may tend to keep people from working in harmony. He or she must be able to accept individuals with differing views, help resolve personal and professional differences, encourage compromise when called for, and keep the staff working in unity toward the primary goals of the school. These skills require a sensitive person who possesses a knowledge of psychology, group dynamics, and communication.

Well, there it is; a picture of the super principal. Of course, there are few, if any, who can fill the bill of the ideal school administrator. Much is expected and much is required of any person placed in charge of the education of our children. It takes a dedicated person to be a successful Christian-school administrator.

Terminating an Administrator's Services

In times of trouble the administrator must know his or her rights and the wise course to follow. In some principal-board conflicts the "I'd rather fight than switch" attitude dominates. Such an attitude is not beneficial for those involved, for the Christian school, or for Christ's glory. We sometimes lose sight of the fact that we must occasionally take it on the chin for His sake. His counsel to "turn the other cheek" says it best.

This advice to the administrator does not mean that the unfair or stubborn school board has license to do what it will with the worn-out administrator. On the contrary, the board, too, is expected to go the second mile. Occasionally an administrator who has served a Christian school for many years is suddenly notified that he or she is no longer wanted. Usually the board has some vague reason for such action; suddenly the matter has become urgent and cannot wait. "They told me they heard complaints," one administrator said. "A few just wanted a change," explained another. Others say, "They felt I was not giving any leadership," or, "They said there was not enough order in the school."

Administrators would do well to remember that they work for the school at the behest of the school board. The board has the final word on whether the administrator is doing the job or not, and it also can tell the administrator that it is time to move on. Usually length of service—even length of faithful service—will not deter a board if it is convinced that the school is being held back or being negatively affected by an administrator. After all, that is the board's prerogative. A wise administrator, then, does not rest on the oars; if the ship is sinking, he or she abandons the ship before it goes under. If the administrator goes under with the public fully aware of his or her plight, the future (for both administrator and school) may be unnecessarily turbulent.

The board must do all in its power to avoid public disgrace of a faithful servant. Much too often the board pats itself on the back for taking on a tough job or doing what had to be done. Generally this is nonsense. After all, firing an administrator is not to be equated with some display of manliness or with sharp business practices. If the board really feels the administrator is a detriment to the school, it must take action to remove him or her from that position. The big question is *how* such action should be carried out.

All of us can name at least one administrator who does not have what it takes to be an administrator. Most of those people who fall into the category know they are marginal in their administrative ability. Some leave the profession without any push at all. Others cling to the hope that things will get better. Such an administrator constantly fights the fear that the board will eventually realize how much difficulty he or she is in, and how inadequate he or she is in coping with it. What these people may need is merely to have someone sit down and level with them.

A former administrator confessed, "I was miserable as a principal. I knew I wasn't doing the job well. I saw so many others who were much better at it. When the board president asked me if I was really happy in my work, I said no. He suggested I might be happier in a different job and I agreed. I *am* happier in my new job and I feel I do it well."

Some marginal administrators are not as objective about their effectiveness. They reason, "If they were satisfied with my work for the past ten years, why not now?" They blame the school board—usually the board president—for the present state of dissatisfaction. Of course, school boards change and most schools require a different type of leadership today than they did ten years ago. School boards have come to expect dynamic progress in their schools, a will to improve, and an administrator who leads rather than rests. Yet some administrators resist change; they are in a deep rut and can't seem to get even halfway out.

What does the school board owe the administrator who has served them faithfully in the past but who, they now conclude, can no longer fill their expectations? They owe him or her the opportunity for a gracious way out. If an administrator has served for a number of years, one more year is not going to ruin the school. The first step in the separation of a faithful servant should be a heart-to-heart talk between the administrator and one or more of the board leaders. Step two may be a heart-to-heart talk between the administrator and the executive committee of the board, at which time the needs of the school and of the administrator are explored. An older administrator may be only too relieved to leave his post, but he or she has to make a living—and most schools are not waiting with open arms for those who are over fifty. Any school board of ten or twelve members ought to have someone with business connections who can assist the administrator in finding a new occupation if he or she needs one.

If the board shows a sensitivity to the trauma of the released administrator, and tries to help relieve that trauma, it can often find an amiable arrangement. Time to adjust, to search for a job, and to talk the situation out, is essential if the separation is going to be made as painlessly as possible. This means that the board must not suddenly "lower the boom" some spring evening and let the administrator wander home in a state of shock.

Some administrators just will not face up to the inevitable. The wise administrator begins to consider other choices when the board begins to have doubts about his or her ability to serve well. He or she does not bury his or her head in the sand and merely hope. Occasionally an administrator recognizes the signs of dissatisfaction and vows to improve. Some accomplish that goal, ride out the discontent, and retire in style. However, that is the exception rather than the rule. When parents are unhappy with the school and/or the administrator, and the board begins to make threatening noises, a wise administrator begins to look for an exit. He or she may sense that a basic injustice and lack of appreciation for his or her efforts are involved, but the situation will not change. If the administrator is realistic about the situation and the board is sensitive about letting him or her down easily and without disgrace, the separation of an administrator from his or her job need not be traumatic for the person involved or damaging to the school or to the Christian name it bears.

Selecting an Administrator

Let us assume that you are an administrator, ready to move to a position of greater responsibility. You apply for a position which you feel is made to order for you. Its challenges are completely in accord with your training and experience. Of course it would be ideal if you could simply step up and say, "I'm the person you are looking for. When do I start?" But it's not that easy. First, you will likely have to go through the ordeal of the selection process.

The CSI study on changes among administrative personnel discovered that the selection process often leaves much to be desired. Usually it is not conducted with sensitive consideration of the candidates; rather it is designed for the convenience of those who are to make the decision. Perhaps this is understandable, but that does not make it any more bearable for the hapless candidate who bares his soul, only to be rejected. The study revealed that 36 percent of the administrators responding to the survey feel that the selection process used in their hiring was in need of improvement. This is especially significant since one's natural inclination would be to be positive about a selection process which ultimately led to one's own appointment. If 36 percent of the people selected by the process think the process is in need of improvement, then many of those candidates who were *not* selected must be even more disillusioned. We are also led to the conclusion that some turnover of administrative personnel may be a result of an inadequate selection process. One thing is certain: the selection process often does not select the best person for the job.

There are many factors in the selection process which may result in the choice of someone other than the best candidate. The school board or its selection committee often comes to the selection process with preconceived notions. Friendships or a special relationship between one or more members of the selection committee and the candidate may so precondition judgment that the whole process is of no effect. A school board may have determined whom they want as administrator long before any interviews even take place. A strong-willed board member may have insisted that "this is the man" for their school, yet the committee interviewed four candidates. The preselected candidate had the poorest interview by far, but he was selected.

There is nothing wrong with a school board's selecting someone it wants because it knows him or her to be suitable; however, it is highly inconsiderate of the board to go through a complete selection process when the outcome, for all intents and purposes, has been predetermined. Such circumstances drive good candidates from the field and encourage third-rate (or worse) candidates to try to get the job.

If an administrative position is going to be offered to the best candidate, then an honest, nonpolitical effort must be made to determine who is the most capable candidate. The integrity of the selection process must be maintained; for a Christian school nothing less will ever do.

If everything is in order and the school board really wants the best principal it can get, what elements should be included in the selection process? First, the school board should develop a good plan for the selection of its administrator. In developing a plan of action the board should consider the following:

1. The goals of the school system should be clearly in mind—preferably on paper—so that the administrator selected will have similar goals.
2. A time schedule for the selection process should be developed so that the school does not lose good candidates because it is too late.
3. Criteria for selection should be carefully chosen. What qualifications are needed for the job? The

board should not hem itself in with needless restrictions, but neither should it set its sights too low regarding professional training and experience.

4. The board should determine what preference, if any, will be given to present staff members or to those who have served the school well in the past.

5. The board should decide with whom it will consult in compiling a list of candidates.

6. A decision should be made concerning how and to what degree present staff members will be involved in the selection process. Situations have developed where every staff member agreed on a certain candidate but the board completely ignored this consensus of staff opinion and selected someone else. If a board is to involve staff, it need not follow the staff's recommendations; but it should not involve the staff at all if it does not intend to consider the staff's opinions seriously. Merely going through the motions will not fool an alert staff. Staff morale and performance will suffer as a result, and the new principal will have to struggle with a resentment hard to overcome.

7. The board should determine how *it* will be involved in the process. Will it interview candidates or leave that to a screening committee? Will it merely give its final stamp of approval? Will it actually do some of the final screening itself?

8. A policy statement concerning the role of the administrator should be on hand. Exactly what position is this person being asked to fill? Some boards are so hesitant to give up administrative prerogatives that they do not even want to call their superintendent or principal by that title. They sometimes prefer titles like "manager," "administrative assistant," or "director of operations." The role of the administrator and the expectations of the board should be clearly spelled out so that an

administrator does not accept a position which he or she later finds does not really exist.

9. In evaluating the candidates a uniform rating sheet should be used. In this way, the members of the board will know what is being looked for and will have some definite areas in which to make comparisons. This is preferable to falling back on impressions. Usually the last candidate interviewed is the best remembered. Evaluation by oral consensus is often evaluation by peer persuasion. In such cases one person with a strong personal interest can outlast those with lesser will power and, in effect, select an administrator for the school. Too many times inferior candidates have been selected by the domination of one person on the committee. Every one loses in such cases.

10. The board should plan for financial considerations. Bringing in out-of-town candidates will make demands on the budget. The board should also have a salary or, at least, a salary range in mind.

Announcing the Opening

When the selection plan is complete, the board is ready to find the best person for the job. In this effort the board should then take the following actions:

1. The board should announce the opening in order that all possible candidates may be aware that an administrator is needed.

2. The board should develop a screening committee. This committee should have the confidence of all board members. The committee will review all the applications and will check out the references of those who look promising.

3. The board should require that the screening committee report with the names of those candidates that should be interviewed. This list will contain

only the names of those who the committee feels
could adequately fill the position. The screening
committee should not designate a preference for one
candidate above all others, because such a process
will prejudice the school board. If one candidate truly
does stand out, that should become evident to the
board during the interview process. Presenting a slate
of candidates from which the board selects in open
session is less susceptible to individual politics and/or
any resulting suspicions.

Interviewing Procedures

The school board now must make its decision regarding
whom it will appoint. The decision-making process should
involve at least the following elements:

1. The board ought to agree on the interview procedures—such things as time, place, role of the board,
   and who will contact the candidates.
2. All interviews should occur within a short time
   span—no more than a day or two apart, but not one
   interview right after another. Some boards like to
   interview during lunch or dinner because candidates
   are often more at ease and board members can get
   a better look at personality and style.
3. The interview is a two-way street, allowing the candidate to get a picture of the school and the position,
   and allowing the board to get a view of the candidate.
4. Specific questions should be asked of all candidates,
   with notes kept of the answers. These questions
   should cover personal goals and accomplishments,
   administrative experiences, and views on a range of
   matters such as curriculum development, evaluation, discipline, professional improvement, and basic
   philosophy.
5. The board should make a judgment as to whether
   the candidate displays clarity of thought and an

ability to communicate ideas in the interview. Glibness should not be mistaken for knowledge or good judgment, but inability to communicate well is a definite drawback for any administrator.

6. Personality can be both overrated and underrated. A person with a pleasant manner will likely work better with children and staff. On the other hand, a pleasant smile or voice is not an adequate substitute for knowledge or administrative ability.

7. After the candidate and board members have been given an opportunity to ask questions, the candidate should be thanked and informed as to when a decision will be reached and how he or she will be informed concerning the decision. The candidates should be the first to know the board's decision.

8. The board should review with each candidate the salary and fringe-benefit package the school is offering. This will allow the candidate to ask questions and to inform the board as to his or her financial needs. It will also allow the board to determine beforehand if the candidate is likely to accept the position if it is offered.

Appointment Procedures

When the decision has been made, the selected candidate should be contacted first. If he or she indicates that acceptance of the appointment is likely, the other candidates also should be notified immediately. If reasonable doubt exists regarding the appointee's decision, the board may wish to delay notifying the other candidates a few days. This will allow the board to appoint another candidate if their first choice declines the appointment. It is incumbent on the selected candidate to notify the board immediately after he or she reaches a decision. In no case should the other candidates be left waiting longer than necessary after the interview process. Staff and constituents should then be notified immediately.

The Transition Process

The transition process need not be difficult for an incoming administrator if consideration is shown by the departing administrator, the staff, and the school board. An early meeting between the new and the departing administrators is essential. It should be clearly understood what matters for the approaching school year will be tended to by the present administrator. Such matters as staff assignments, schedules, and the ordering of materials should be considered. A review of the staff members' abilities and performance will also be helpful. Administrative matters which are in the process of development or which need to be reviewed, weaknesses in the educational program, unique problems with students or constituents, and suggestions for improvements would surely be classified as important information for the newly-appointed administrator.

The staff and board must offer wholehearted cooperation and support to the new administrator. Surely the key to a good start is a good relationship with all who have a role in the school. It is not inappropriate for the administrator to ask for information and for the support needed to get him or her and the school off to a good start. The administrator is not the only person responsible for the success of the school. All school-board members and staff members share in that responsibility, and are usually more than willing to do their part to see that the new person in charge is successful.

2

The Board in Action

The administrator and the school board must work effectively together as a team to provide the best possible framework for a sound educational program within the school or system. This means that an effective method of communication must be established. It should be clear to a responsible administrator that he or she must take the initiative for establishing such communication. The board cannot operate effectively without adequate information, nor can it communicate its position to the staff without prior good communication with the administrator.

The system of communication between the administrator and the board cannot be left to happenstance. It must be established through an understanding effort by both parties. The development of good communication must be a priority item on the agenda at an early meeting between the board and the new administrator. In this meeting they should discuss the most effective means for keeping the board and staff informed concerning all operational aspects of the school or system, and concerning any problems that may arise. The administrator should explore with the board those areas of concern about which the board wishes him or her to regularly report. At this meeting the administrator and board should develop procedures, understanding, and an atmosphere of cooperation. The procedures will vary from school to school depending on size and location.

In a Christian school the administrator and the board should feel an equal responsibility for the establishment of mutual trust and understanding. That is the essence of good communication. Once this atmosphere is established, the way is clear for meaningful interchange of ideas; when a breakdown in communication does occur, it will be overcome by the mutual regard each party has for the other.

One can readily see that this need for mutual regard between board and administrator precludes communicating negative judgments of the board and the administrator (including their decisions) to the staff or to members of the community. Such actions, either by the administrator or by board members, will tend to reduce effective cooperation.

The administrator should share with the board his information, ideas, and positions when the board is trying to reach a decision. The administrator should make known exactly how he or she views the problem and what he or she feels to be appropriate action. Once a vote is taken, win or lose, the administrator takes the board's decision as his or her mandate. A board can understandably lose patience with any administrator who publicly disagrees with board decisions. Privately, with board members, the administrator should feel free to express personal opinions, but publicly the administrator must support and carry out the board's decision.

On rare occasions a board decision may be so distasteful to an administrator that he or she simply cannot be a party to it. In such circumstances the administrator should frankly state his or her position to the board. The board may then set guidelines for him or her, excuse him or her from a role in carrying out the decision, or ask the administrator to resign if the board's mandate cannot be fulfilled.

Relationships Between Board Officers and Administrator

The Christian-school administrator and the board president share a unique relationship. The board president is usually the administrator's official point of contact with the board. If the administrator wishes to report a matter to the board outside of a board meeting, he or she merely contacts the board president. Once that contact is made, the administrator may conclude that the board has been informed concerning the matter.

The board president also may speak to the administrator on behalf of the board. If the administrator brings a problem to the board president and is given a verbal "green light," he or she may proceed as if the school board had given approval. It is the responsibility of the board president to judge whether the green light may be given without consultation with the entire board. Of course, the sensitive administrator will help the board president determine whether it is prudent to proceed with or without consultation with others. It does not serve the school or the administrator well if the board becomes resentful of the assumption of authority by the board president and the administrator.

The administrator must be aware that the position of the board president can also be put in jeopardy. A school board usually will go along at least once with an administrator and board president who overstep good judgment in exercising authority, providing that authority is not used as a means of circumventing the board's will. The wise administrator does not needlessly put the board president on the spot, and the wise board president will not take individual action unless time and circumstances make it necessary.

The administrator also assists the board president in his or her responsibility for conducting the board meeting. The authority for operating the school rests with the board. The board can make decisions only when it is in session. Therefore, the board's meeting time must be used well; the administrator can be of much help in planning productive board meetings.

The board president often depends on the administrator to help in developing the agenda for the meeting. Important matters should be placed early on the agenda so they will not be crowded out by lack of time to consider them adequately. The administrator and board president should discuss the procedures to be followed by the chairman in conducting the meeting. The administrator can inform the chairman of possible problem areas which may arise. Together they should plan the best techniques for handling questions which may surface. They should discuss matters which relate to the agenda. The administrator should indicate the items on which he or she would like to speak, and what kind of reports or information will be given to the board members. The chairman should be made aware if staff members or interested constituents are to appear. He or she should know what, if any, correspondence is to be presented. In other words, there should be no surprises at board meetings.

The administrator must also work to maintain rapport with the other board officers and members. He or she should take every precaution to treat each board member alike. Each board member has one vote. Thus, when it comes to board decisions, the vote of the least capable or least friendly board member is equal to that of the most capable and the most supportive board member. Some administrators have made themselves feel comfortable and accepted by becoming a part of a clique within the board. Such a situation has within it the seeds of dissension and self-destruction. However, the administrator's unique relationship with the board chairman is usually understood by other board members and will not be resented if it is not overdone.

Relationships Between Board and Staff

Most administrators still cling to a basic philosophy of administration which considers the administrator as the communicator between board and staff. Administrators are uneasy, even resentful, when board members bypass them to deal directly with staff members. Conversely, administrators are equally resentful if staff members bypass them and go directly to board members. It is not difficult to understand the administrator's dislike of being bypassed. Staff members may find that board members are sometimes more receptive to certain proposals than is the administrator; after all, it is the administrator who often has to live with and defend the decision, while the board member can simply be the agreeable party who says yes.

Those who indulge in bypassing proper channels are playing a dangerous game. Reason takes a holiday and politics can take the front seat when the administrator is regularly bypassed. Decisions are no longer made on the basis of the effect they may have on the school system or of what is best for all, but rather on the basis of who can be most easily convinced. Often the administrator must say no to a proposal when he or she would much prefer to say yes. He sees the future and the broader implications of the decision, implications that others with more limited vision or responsibility do not see. It is therefore the better part of wisdom to preserve the role of the administrator as the communicator between staff and board.

Administrators sometimes wonder how they can deal with the board member who contacts individual staff members for opinions or information. The administrator should bring the matter to the board president and encourage a conference with the offending board member, or speak to the whole board concerning the problems produced when there is direct contact with the staff. Of course, the administrator can also talk to the offending board member personally and point out these problems. Another approach would be to advise all staff members how to properly handle a board member who contacts them. Certainly, the staff member must be courteous and listen to the problem which the board member poses. The staff member should then invite the board member to accompany him or her to the administrator to present the problem. This enables the staff member to assist the board member without usurping the role of the administrator and, possibly, raising his or her ire.

Problems of communication usually do not exist where there is a climate of mutual trust and respect. The board member should be able to talk with staff members and staff members with board members without peering over their shoulders for fear that the administrator may appear. Unless the administrator is faced with a specific problem generated by an indiscretion of a member of the board or staff, an open and continuing relationship must be fostered between staff and board. A framework must be provided for effective two-way communication, so that staff and board members have access to each other through the administrator's office and person.

The administrator is in the unique position of liaison between board and staff. This position carries with it the responsibility to orient new board and staff members to accepted procedures in communication between staff and board, staff and administrator, and board and administrator. It is impossible to overstate the importance of this period of orientation. Long-standing attitudes are often learned in the first year of service on the board and on the staff.

Orienting New Staff and Board Members

Usually only the administrator is in a position to help new staff members and board members form the correct attitudes so that they will understand what constitutes acceptable communication procedures. Because of the important role the administrator has in getting new staff and board members off on the right foot, it may be beneficial to give a brief overview of the orientation period and the points the administrator should emphasize during it:

1. The administrator must assure the board and the staff members that their personal inquiries are welcome concerning any aspect of the school's operation. When these people do appear with a question, whatever time is needed should be taken to fully answer it.
2. The administrator should initiate orientation sessions with new staff and board members where procedures and relationships are openly discussed. Remember, new people are usually reluctant to take much initiative in the early stages of their service.
3. Orientation may well include a visit of board members to the classrooms and the principal's office. Each staff and board member should become familiar with office procedures and personnel. This will help to smooth the avenues of communication.
4. The board member should learn how to best channel his or her concerns. He or she should know which problems are to be brought to the board, which to the administrator, which to the board president, and which to a staff member. Each board member should understand how to get matters on the board agenda, how to handle complaints from parents or others, and how to initiate a desired action.
5. Board members should be helped to understand why it is unwise in most cases for them to bypass the administrator in contacting staff members. Not only does this put staff members on the spot; it also subjects them to the whims of a number of people whose position in relation to them is often unclear.
6. Staff members must see the rationale for making contacts with board members through or at least with the knowledge of the administrator. No admin-

istrator appreciates it when at a board meeting a board member quotes or refers to a staff member as the source of his or her information. The administrator must know what is coming up or is likely to come up in the board meeting, and he or she should know the staff's concerns regarding those matters. Leaving the administrator uninformed could, and often does, result in an inability or lack of desire to help the cause. Additionally, it is a matter of considerateness and good ethics not to exclude the administrator of a school in solving the wide range of school problems.

7. Some staff members become very uneasy or angry when an administrator entertains a parent's complaint about them without first insisting that the parent communicate with the teacher involved. Of course, the administrator should ask whether the parent has shared the concerns with the teacher, and should encourage the parent to do so. However, the administrator serves the parent, too. He or she cannot refuse to discuss a problem merely because the parent did not follow the best line of procedure. Usually it takes a lot of soul-searching before a parent gets up the courage to speak to the administrator about a matter in the first place. If the administrator refuses to listen for any reason, the parent becomes puzzled, discouraged, even angry. The staff, the board member, and the administrator must always be willing to communicate with all persons concerned with the school. They should not pass immediate judgments on matters brought to them, but they should promise that the appropriate person will be contacted, and that the matter will receive proper attention. Usually a follow-up report is made to the concerned party.

8. The administrator is the board's agent and acts on behalf of the board in all matters pertaining to the

school. No one board member can act as the board's agent unless he or she has specifically been mandated to do so by the whole board. The discretionary authority the board grants the chief administrator usually exceeds the authority of any individual board member. Of course, it is the board which has ultimate authority over the school, its personnel, and its own membership, but that authority can be used only when the board is in session. Staff members must realize, then, that no individual board member may direct them, and the board member must understand the limits of his or her individual authority. Since supervision of the staff is one of the authorities given the administrator by the board, it is the administrator who serves as the agent of the board; the individual board member has no such authority over the staff.

9. The wise board protects and does not undermine the unique relationship that exists between staff members and the administrator. The board gives the administrator specific responsibility as pertains to the staff. The board can hold the administrator responsible for the conduct and performance of the staff. Should the board interfere in that relationship, then it relieves the administrator of some of the responsibility for staff performance. Under such conditions the staff may come to regard the administrator as being without status and thus his or her leadership role is weakened. This weakened role has broad implications regarding the effectiveness of administrator and staff.

The quality of the relationships between staff, board, and administrator has a heavy impact on the spirit and the operation of the school. It is essential, then, that proper methods of communication be clearly understood by all board and staff members.

3

School Climate and School Spirit

What makes one Christian school excellent and another inferior? Why are two schools of equal quality often regarded as being of differing quality? What are the elements which make a school appear to be a quality school? These questions suggest that the perception of quality is often as important to a school as is the fact itself. What fosters a positive perception? What makes the climate in and around a school positive and constructive? What gives a school the spirit which will carry it through good and bad times, and retain the approval of those who know it and use it?

Some have concluded that the administrator is the single most important element in establishing a highly regarded school. A British study (Michael Rutter et al., *Fifteen Thousand Hours*, 1979) concluded that differences among schools depend to a large extent on the administrator's ability to build a supportive, challenging, and positive school climate.

Of course, school climate is more than just a good feeling about a school. It *is* that, but beyond that it includes the participation of everyone connected with the school. Everyone must focus on the school's goals and on helping students reach their full potentials. A school climate includes the personal relationships among pupils, staff, administrator, board, and community.

One can readily see that the leadership and spirit of the administrator are very important in establishing the school's educational climate. Often a cheerful and exciting atmosphere reflects a cheerful and enthusiastic administrator. A staff or student body kept on edge by a negative response to most of the things they do is ultimately going to be affected in *everything* they do. The administrator's negative attitude will be reflected in much of what they feel and say about their school.

There is adequate evidence that students attain more in schools where students and staff get along well together. In a 1977 study, Brookover and Lezatte found that schools which have high student performance also have faculties which agree with the objectives of the school, which have high expectations of their students, and which accept responsibility for achieving the school's goals. On the other hand, schools with low levels of student achievement are characterized by few changes and by an unwillingness to attempt to solve problems, especially when such attempts might upset the status quo. Brookover and Lezatte also found that strong leadership by the administrator is essential to the improvement of school climate.

A good administrator recognizes that his or her role in the school is at least twofold: the school must be administered in a way which will produce educated persons, but in the process an atmosphere must be created which gives the staff and student satisfaction with the process and with their role in it. The staff member has a dual need. He or she wishes to serve the children well but also wants to face each day with optimism and satisfaction in the service given.

Staff morale is the internal attitude of the staff members. Morale is associated with school climate. But these two concepts are not one and the same. It is conceivable that teachers completely lacking in sensitivity and under-standing, as far as students' needs are concerned, may be completely self-satisfied. Morale can be high for the wrong reasons; where staff morale is high, the learning climate of the school can be negative because of a lack of under-standing and sensitivity. Some public-school teachers' unions have become so intent on acquiring teachers' rights that students' needs have been sacrificed. The good ad-ministrator sees to it that the interests of the students are not sacrificed in the name of staff peace or high staff mo-rale. Concern for the Christian-school student must exceed concern for a comfortable and contented faculty. Chris-tian-school teachers understand this, and are usually in the forefront when it comes to sensing and fulfilling stu-dent needs.

The major determiner of the climate of any organiza-tion is its perceived leader. In a school, this is usually the administrator. In the classroom, this leader is the teacher. That is not to say that a negative school climate is auto-matically the administrator's fault. After all, the admin-istrator does not have complete and unfettered control over the school. A school with a normally good climate could suffer because of unwise or inconsiderate actions of the school board. The climate of the classroom could be negatively affected by the presence of one or more difficult students. Such variations in the atmosphere of a school or a classroom dictate varying strategies to achieve cli-mate improvement. The procedures needed for improve-ment may pertain to improving discipline, teacher supervision, interpersonal relationships, or a host of other matters which combine to make up the school's learning and teaching climate. Generally it is the administrator who orchestrates the actions which are needed for im-provement. However, the planning for action involves all who have a stake in the school.

Climate Planning

In planning the climate all those involved with the school must help identify those areas that are of concern. There must be a large circle of persons included in improvement projects. Results will be accomplished without conflict if the focus is placed on desired outcomes rather than on particular means. Certain steps can be taken by the administrator to improve the school's social and learning climate. These steps may include:

1. Setting the goal(s) and determining the ideal climate which the school leadership desires. The effort must be given focus and direction.
2. Determining who is to be included in the improvement or maintenance effort. The climate affects students, parents, board members, teachers, administrators, and the community. It must be decided if the focus is to include all of these or if it is to be more limited.
3. Determining specific areas of concern. Perhaps one or more surveys will be needed to evaluate the present school circumstances and to decide where efforts should be directed.
4. Recognizing that all areas of concern probably cannot be addressed immediately. It will be necessary to establish priorities based on the levels of satisfaction of the parties involved. Teachers may regard as top priority a matter which the board or parents regard as one of lesser concern. Parents, on the other hand, may have a number of concerns to which staff members may give a low priority. Remember, too much variety will lead to confusion and will dissipate the energy and the effort of those who seek to solve the problems. It is essential that the focus be on only two or three problems at any one time. When one problem is satisfactorily solved, another can be

worked on. If the concerned parties have different priorities, select the top priorities of each party as the initial focus.

5. Acquiring information from all available sources pertaining to the area under review. Use those in your community and on your staff, but also use professional resources, such as the personnel of Christian Schools International, colleges, other school systems, or other school service agencies.

6. Selecting a course of action which has a clear goal and a means of reaching it efficiently. It may also be necessary to appoint someone to be responsible for the project.

7. Establishing a schedule for the project. The schedule should be divided into segments for the various phases of the project: organization, information collecting, decision-making, and implementation. Remember, most people will keep their energy high at the beginning of any activity, before the novelty of the effort has worn off. Drive and desire become important as the going gets tough and decisions are hard to make.

8. Proceeding to implement the course of action you have determined. Review results. The process may require changes in action as a lack of desired results or a more demanding need is observed. Do not change directions too often or too soon because benefits will not be gained from a lot of aimless activities. On the other hand, do not continue an effort which is obviously going nowhere.

9. Keeping the communication lines open to all concerned parties and building evaluation procedures into the project. No one will know all the work involved in making improvements unless there is communication with those concerned. No one will realize the value of the project unless a special effort is made to determine the results.

The Leadership Role in Creating School Climate

Some administrators are satisfied to merely organize a project, set it in motion, and sit back and wait for results. Some administrators promote themselves by citing the many projects they have undertaken, ostensibly to improve the school climate. Such administrators often can be found telling an audience what "we" are doing at Action Christian School. There is nothing wrong with sharing ideas and accomplishments with others who may be stimulated by the experience. However, it is not enough for an administrator merely to implement the structure for climate improvement. He or she must also exercise an ongoing leadership role which is needed to assure the long-term effects of climate-improving projects. The administrator cannot act like some far-off deity who sets the world in motion and promptly withdraws himself from the scene.

Effective leadership means that the administrator stays involved and remains aware of conditions and events taking place in the school community. The effective leader is aware of the expectations of others. He or she is alert to any changes that should be made to attain the goals which are sought, and encourages others to work for results. The administrator's encouragement is especially important. In a 1970 study, Brookover and others reported that a sense of futility is a prime cause of lack of achievement in schools and pupils. It follows that an administrator who has realistic expectations and gives encouragement can help stem the sense of futility and promote achievement.

One can readily see the impact of high expectations on a youngster's achievement. The administrator carries a large responsibility for creating a climate of high expectations. He or she can direct the school toward a high level of student productivity and satisfaction by working to improve the climate experienced by the staff. This climate is transmitted to the classroom and the student shares in it. The positive climate of the school spills over into the Christian family and the social environs of the school. Thus the leadership of the administrator can produce a broad range of impacts on the family, church, and the Christian community. Sometimes, a lively, spiritually growing school becomes the catalyst for a lively and spiritually growing Christian community.

Some wonder why Christian-school leadership does not produce more exciting and growth-producing climates. The truth is that the road to a good climate is not always clear or without obstructions. Proposed changes are not always viewed as opportunities for growth. Inertia often works against progress in rejuvenating school climates. Most institutions are bound up in traditions which resist change. This attitude often prevails: "What we have has always been good enough, so why change?"

The existing organizational structure of the Christian school may be a source of local pride. Changes may be seen as criticism of what has been done and of those who prefer to keep things as they are. There is a sort of pride in the way we do things and what that way has accomplished for us. Why change the financial support system of our schools? After all, it has supported us all these years. Who knows what this new system will do? We may be found wanting. Why take a chance?

The standards and fears of certain constituents sometimes cause them to resist change. For example, for years Christian schools have debated the matter of tax benefits for Christian-school parents. Some consider tax benefits for Christian-school parents simply a matter of public justice. Others regard it as an alliance with a not-too-friendly government which may in time charge too high a price in terms of control over Christian schools. According to the latter, such a risk is not worth whatever benefits the school would receive. These sincerely held beliefs impede any attempt to acquire tax help for tuition-paying parents. The feasibility of such action may well depend on the views held by groups within the constituency.

The habits of individuals can also impede efforts to lead the school into beneficial changes. For example, some schools have always conducted an annual fund-raising campaign. There will be those who will seek to maintain that campaign simply because "we have been able to survive until now because of it." Other schools have never had a financial drive. Some in the constituency will use the same arguments *not* to try one. They will say, "We never needed it before and we can get along without it now."

Teachers also can be creatures of habit. A plan to involve mothers as aides for playground or classroom supervision can make teachers uneasy when they have always had the class to themselves. Such teachers are likely to ask, "Why are they needed? I can handle my class alone." Yet when these same people once become accustomed to regular help in the classroom, they can become enthusiastic advocates of the program. Old habits die hard but good leadership can help people step out into new areas and conquer any discomfort and fears.

Change is best accomplished when those who will be affected by it are involved in initiating and implementing it. Good leaders give credit for change to those most involved in bringing it about. Good leaders refer to a new program as the "teachers' program" or the "board's program" rather than "my program." A good leader always remembers that the best ideas are credited to someone else and that enlightened self-interest is a major motivator for change. Credit, praise, self-interest, and service are the elements which stimulate the climate of a good school.

The person in charge is the primary influence on the climate of any organization. In the eyes of most persons connected with the school, the administrator is accountable for what happens in the school. Satisfaction with the school is seen as a direct or indirect result of the administrator's leadership.

Even though the teacher establishes the climate within a classroom, the students and teachers usually expect that the administrator can and should reward good teachers and correct or replace poor teachers. Teachers expect their good performance to be noticed and in some way rewarded by the administrator. When staff and students are satisfied with the environment of the school and perceive the school as meeting their expectations, the administrator is usually described as a good one. If the constituents also have a positive perception of the school, the administrator is well on the way to being a success.

There is also a need for a healthy climate for the administrator. He or she can become so much involved in serving others that family and personal spiritual needs are neglected. The administrator may have so many responsibilities and concerns that he or she carries the weight of those responsibilities through every waking hour. Some administrators have found these demands too cumbersome; they have sought to escape the burden by changing professions. While setting a proper climate for the school and others who work there, the administrator must not be unconcerned about the needs of self and family.

In a recent study, the National Association of Secondary School Principals found that administrators place a strong emphasis on environmental conditions in the school. These conditions fall into four categories: emotional environment, social environment, sense of purpose, and cognitive environment. Administrators are also interested in aiming at certain goals which they believe contribute in turn to a positive school climate. These goals include student achievement, development of self-concept, changes in behavior, and changes in attitude. No doubt, if this study had been conducted among Christian-school administrators, service to God and man would be high on the list of goals.

The totality of the leadership challenges faced by any administrator can be overwhelming. That is why the task must be broken down into manageable components. The administrator must avoid the sort of pessimism felt when facing a mountain with a shovel. He or she must also be aware of the pitfalls of unwarranted enthusiasm for a particular fad or approach to problems.

In order to get a handle on controlling school climate, the administrator must realize that his or her major role is dealing with the staff. He or she provides the staff with information, inspiration, support, and supervision so they can better carry out their part in the program. They become the vehicle for the realization of the administrator's expectations. The administrator can transmit to the staff a sense of complacency or a sense of urgency. If the administrator is optimistic and organized, the staff is likely to emulate those characteristics. Additionally, the staff will tend to pass on its optimism to the students and to the constituency.

Many administrators do not realize the extent of their influence on the direction and climate of the school. Often the spirit of the school is a mirror image of the spirit of the administrator. If the administrator is easygoing, the staff and in turn the student will reflect a similar attitude. If the administrator is defensive and restrictive, the staff and student body often become tense.

One can readily see why the administrator must know himself or herself. An alert administrator can compensate for some personal characteristics. If he or she is inclined to be low-key, it may be wise to look for staff members who are more intense. If the administrator tends to be easygoing, staff members, office help, or assistants who are more demanding should be sought. Everyone has certain strengths and weaknesses. A good administrator recognizes the strengths and weaknesses of others and adjusts his or her administrative style to use them in a way that will contribute to a positive school climate.

4

Improving the School Staff

Teachers have feelings, too. That fact is firmly set in the mind of any good administrator. The teacher brings a number of professional and personal goals to the classroom. In a sense he or she is on a search for meaning in work and in life. The teacher may have his or her goals worked out well or may be merely groping for meaning. Spiritually, the teacher should know the source and object of faith, and should make it manifest to others, particularly the students and colleagues. Jesus should be the dominant person and force in the teacher's life. Where there is meaning, there is conviction; a good teacher has both.

There is great diversity among teachers. All teachers do not have a clear vision. Some are working to get in tune with their Lord, or they may need some fine adjustment to get a clearer perspective of the spiritual path for their lives.

Another element which enters the picture is the desire to teach, or lack of such desire. Some people seem to fall into teaching and have difficulty in answering the question, "Why did you become a teacher?" They are unsure of their professional choice. They may once have thought they would love to work with children only to find that children can be difficult to work with. Do they really want

to make teaching their lifetime career? Some cannot give
a clear answer to that question.

There are also personal aspirations and goals—mar-
riage, a home, a family—to consider. And there is money.
What style of life do teachers visualize for themselves?
Teaching will not make them well-to-do. It will not give
them an easy financial road. So what *do* they want out of
life? Will Christian-school teaching help them reach their
spiritual, professional, and personal goals?

The good administrator reckons with these variables in
the lives of teachers. He or she helps the teacher in the
search for meaning in life. In a real sense the administrator is counselor and guide to the teaching staff. The good
administrator is not so deeply involved in his or her own
personal problems that the problems, worries, and cares
of staff members cannot be sensed; he or she is one of
their guides in the search to find meaning in all that they
do.

People who have a firmly established faith tend to forget the struggles they experienced when their faith was
new. Many young people who enter teaching may be ex-
periencing doubts and uncertainties about their faith in
the Lord. Those who have been brought up in Christian
homes have been schooled in particular attitudes about
religion. They may have a guilty feeling about their doubts
and their concerns. Perhaps they are only going through
the motions of a religious person without actually expe-
riencing the presence of God in their hearts and in their
lives.

Those who have discovered salvation and a life in Christ
have also discovered a profound and intimate personal
meaning in their profession and life. Their goal is to help
others make the same discovery through God's Word and
creation.

The administrator, aware of the struggles in the lives
of teachers, tries to establish a climate and an atmosphere
where their thoughts and fears can be freely expressed.

The administrator helps teachers in their effort to face themselves.

Staff Development

Every administrator should have a program for staff development. The teacher is the heart of any educational system; thus the staff-development program will to a great extent determine the quality of the school. Usually it is the school leadership which determines the nature, mode, and extent of the growth of the school's staff. The leader's role is to be an example to the staff, to exhort the staff with respect to mutual concerns, and to formulate and implement speedy remedies to problems.

The first task of any administrator is to size up the staff. For example, ask yourself some of these questions:

What are the capabilities of the staff members?

Are they presently able to meet any challenges they may face?

How do the staff members feel about themselves and about each other?

Are there any problems with personal relationships?

Can they, will they, work well together?

Are there certain people who do not seem to fit or who may cause intrastaff problems?

Are some inclined to work against the leadership? Why?

Are they willing to express their true feelings?

Are they willing to contribute to and share with each other?

Do they have empathy for each other?

Does the group interact well within itself? Is there good-natured banter?

Is the staff professionally alert?

Do they seek to find the best methods and materials? Or do they rest on past practices?

Do they know and understand the administrator's and board's expectations of them?

Are they sensitive to children and to parents?

What are their academic capabilities? Can and will these capabilities be shared?

These are some questions an alert administrator will ask. The usefulness of knowing the staff as individuals and as a group is obvious.

Expectations

An administrator can know the staff well and yet not get maximum benefit from that knowledge. Many administrators fail in efforts to improve the educational program of their school because they do not fully involve the teacher in the fabric of the school. Administrators seem to leave the teacher in the classroom and the problems in their office.

Teachers know that students will adjust their responses to what they perceive the teacher wants from them. If a teacher rewards them for a word-for-word response taken from a book, that is the type of response that teacher will tend to generate. Similarly, if a teacher rewards a student for creative thinking apart from what the book says, that teacher will tend to generate that type of effort and response from the students.

Teachers are not unlike their students in this regard. If the administrator tends to praise and reward splashy bulletin boards and twenty little seats in nice neat rows, that is what some teachers will tend to give, whether or not they consider it beneficial for good education.

This means that an administrator should have clearly

in mind what is important in Christian education and should communicate it well to the teachers; otherwise, the teachers should be left to decide what is important. For example, if the administrator ignores or even demeans educational research, one would hardly expect that the teachers are going to take research seriously in their teaching. Even as the teacher's expectations of a student will inevitably affect that student's performance, so, too, what the teacher perceives to be the administrator's expectations will affect the teacher's performance.

There is a parallel between an administrator's understanding of the teacher's problems and a teacher's understanding of the student's problems. It is important to know how an administrator views his teachers and how the teacher views the administrator—even as it is important to know how a student views a teacher and how a teacher views the student. In both cases frank discussions about expectations are needed. The teachers remembered most fondly are those who told the students exactly what was expected of them and without wavering steered them toward meeting those expectations. The administrator discusses great and small expectations with teachers in faculty sessions. The teachers respond by expressing their expectations of themselves, the school, and the administrator. Open discussion without fear of retribution gives the school a healthy climate and stimulates real educational quality.

Rewards of Teaching

Boards and administrators face a quandary concerning the rewarding of those teachers who have exceptional skills. Many businesses promote and reward people on the basis of demonstrated competence. Schools generally pay teachers on the basis of credits earned and years on the job. Although one can safely assume that credits and experience add up to knowledge, one cannot assume that accumulation of knowledge guarantees effective transferral of that knowledge to students. A number of questions should be asked at this point: Which teachers have the best ability to teach? Which teachers most influence the student? Who on the staff best stimulates children to learn? The answers to these questions do not necessarily relate to what the teacher knows. Some of the most brilliant people in the world are not good teachers.

Administrators and boards cannot always be satisfied by the best a teacher has to offer. They have a responsibility to the children placed in their care, and there are times when a teacher's best is not good enough. In those situations the administrator must conduct a detailed firsthand evaluation and report his findings and recommendations to the board. It is difficult to dismiss a person who is not up to the task given him or her, but this is one of the responsibilities of the administrator and he or she must see that it is met.

The teacher's rewards for service in a Christian school are many and varied: the satisfaction of influencing a child for good; of seeing him or her blossom in spirit and in mind; words of appreciation (sometimes years later); the progress and accomplishments of students; the opportunity of serving the Lord in the classroom and seeing Him become meaningful in the lives of the children; the knowledge that one is playing a responsible role in God's plan and in His kingdom; and the privilege of earning one's livelihood by service. These are all inherent rewards of teaching; but, like everything else in life, one must sincerely want to teach in order to do it well.

A word about expressing appreciation is in order. President Reagan is said to have a motto in his office which reads: "A person can accomplish anything if he doesn't mind who gets credit for it." When it comes to schools, it is the teachers that deserve the credit; a good administrator and a good board see to it that they get it.

Improving Teacher Effectiveness

One can learn to cook by carefully following certain techniques and recipes. A good cook follows these techniques and recipes with care; a bad cook does not. A salesperson can learn certain tried and true sales techniques in a relatively short time. Selling is complicated by the variety of personalities among salespeople and among customers. It is not enough merely to know the best sales techniques if one is to be a good salesman, or to follow a cookbook if one is to be a good cook. Similarly, it is not enough to know all of the best teaching techniques if one is to be a good teacher. A good teacher has a sensitivity to the reactions of children. He or she can read a child's signals and sense immediately when there is understanding, desire, despair, or resentment.

Even as the cook or salesman must be a good technician to be successful, so, too, the teacher must know well the laws of learning and how to apply them. It is immediately evident to the alert administrator that all teachers are not equally prepared. The degree of teacher effectiveness varies greatly, just as do student's learning abilities. Consequently, the administrator is faced with the difficult task of somehow matching the teacher's effectiveness with the students' learning abilities. This is done in part by carefully considering teacher and student class assignments and in part by in-service programs for teachers.

Judicious teacher assignments and educational programming can go a long way toward matching teacher abilities and student needs. Such a process requires a flexible use of staff members which makes the right teacher available to the student who needs him or her most. There are three avenues a careful administrator may follow to improve teacher effectiveness: making the best possible use of existing talent, introducing in-service training where most needed, and adjusting school-program patterns to achieve maximum interaction between teacher and child.

The problem of improving teacher effectiveness often seems so great that an administrator will just throw up his or her hands in despair and let matters run their own course. It is surely easier to take the staff you get, assign them, and hope things work out well. Such an attitude is sometimes justified by the proclamation, "I don't get many complaints about my teachers." The assumption is that if people are not complaining, things are going well. But concerned administrators do not rest on such slim evidence of learning or teaching effectiveness.

If the administrator has a mind to seek improvement in teaching effectiveness, what part of the educational machine is repaired first? Most often the efforts to improve teaching in a school begin with an assessment of the needs of the teachers and sometimes the needs of students. A complete assessment of needs can be a major undertaking in itself. It can involve parents, board members, students, teachers, church leadership, and administrators. There is no standard approach to follow. The art of assessing educational needs is not very well developed. That is why the words "assessment of needs" can throw cold water on the whole effort of improving effectiveness. Staff members may say, "We are too busy teaching to get so deeply involved in a large research project like this." They are probably right. Too often an assessment of needs takes up so much time and energy that when it is completed, the first step in the improvement of teaching becomes the last step, too. A thorough list of needs sits on the administrator's desk just being stared at.

But an assessment of needs does not have to be the cumbersome procedure it has often been made out to be. A broad outline of needs arranged in a relative order of importance can be drawn up in one board meeting and one staff meeting. Ask the board members to identify the needs of the school, of the staff, and of the children. Arrange the list in order of greatest to lesser needs. Use a similar approach in the staff meeting. Then combine the two lists. This can be done by the administrator and board president, or some other small group. Now the administrator at least has a guide as to what other people feel the school needs.

The next task of the administrator and the staff is to relate student needs to teacher needs. Charles Silberman in *Crisis in the Classroom* makes the point that teaching and learning are not parts of the same process:

> Without changing the ways in which schools operate and teachers teach, changing the curriculum alone does not have much effect. . . . [Curriculum reformers of the 1960s] somehow assumed that students would learn what teachers taught; that is, if teachers presented the material in the proper structure, students would learn it that way. Thus, they assumed implicitly that teaching and learning are merely opposite sides of the same coin. But they are not.

If Silberman is correct, and no doubt there is some truth in what he says, we will need to determine how teachers can better relate to students in a way which can accomplish the objectives of the curriculum. We will need to sharpen staff competencies in dealing with all kinds of children at many different levels. This puts the finger on the reason teachers are paid according to a schedule weighted heavily on the basis of experience. It takes ten, twelve, or fourteen years for a teacher to reach the top of the salary schedule, but it takes a lifetime to discover the right button to each of the large variety of personalities a teacher faces every day, every year. In teaching, experience *is* the best teacher. One does not learn to adapt to the many shadings of student needs by way of the college classroom or textbook.

Of course, this process can be accelerated by an in-service program which relies heavily on other teachers who have had more and different experiences, and who know how to relate the lessons they have learned in a meaningful way to those who have a need to know. Since the needs of teachers vary, an in-service program must have variety in it. The program must be designed for those who have needs in the areas of instructional techniques, curriculum development, student control, motivation, and performance. There are many purposes for an in-service program:

1. All teachers need to extend their general knowledge. An educated person has a basic interest in and knowledge of an array of topic areas. Teachers come to their profession with varied backgrounds and knowledge. The conscientious teacher knows where weaknesses lie and will seek to fill the gap. This can be accomplished in a number of ways, not the least of which is learning from one's colleagues.

2. Knowledge is increasing at a rapid rate and is constantly undergoing reinterpretation. Therefore, a teacher cannot rest on previously acquired knowledge. A college major in a particular subject area may be inadequate preparation to teach that subject only a few years after graduation. In certain subject areas, for example, science and mathematics, constant updating is critical.

3. The demands of society and of the church on the Christian school are expanding. The Christian-school teacher faces new challenges in the form of demands for applying the Christian philosophy in a meaningful way, for excellence in instruction, and for responding to new and special interests. There is a need for new preparation to meet these challenges.

4. The demands of society carry over into new techniques, materials, and technology. We are faced today with a huge variety of communication devices which can and should become classroom tools. There

are educational innovations which seem to stimulate certain groups of students. The rate of new dis-
coveries is startling and continuous. New and old
ideas in teaching reading, such as "Words in Color,"
the "Initial Teaching Alphabet," and the various applications of phonics, illustrate the many methods
available to today's teachers in just one teaching
area. These ideas and variety of methods will have
no effect in the classrooms unless teachers know of
them and use them to improve their classroom
teaching.

5. A teacher should welcome the challenge of a new
teaching assignment from time to time. These
changes are professionally stimulating. A teacher
benefits from an occasional change of assignment.
A part of the purpose of the in-service program should
be to prepare the teacher for the excitement and
pleasure of teaching a new subject or a different
grade level. The anticipation of rethinking and re-
writing a teaching program will be professionally
stimulating for one who cherishes the challenges of
teaching. (Some teachers may even feel the pull of
supervisory or administrative roles in the school.
Reaching these goals may require a variety of studies, courses, and degrees. Although such a goal is a
worthy personal aim, it should be considered as secondary to the goal of increased teaching competence.)

6. We live in an age of specialization. Teaching, too, has
in some ways become a profession of specialists.
There are those who are specialists in remedial
learning or remedial reading, bilingual programs,
curriculum, early childhood education, adult education, child development, social and community
contacts; the list goes on and becomes longer each
passing year. Each of these areas offers a new hori-
zon and a new challenge to a teacher. One need not
leave the classroom to specialize in an area of inter-

est; on the other hand, if the specialization leads one
to a different professional goal, so be it.

The effective in-service program has two basic aspects.
First, it will involve some elements which all the staff
members have in common and which they can work on
together. Second, it will provide for individuality, so that
each teacher, with as much assistance as he or she needs,
can plan and execute his or her own program. In the first
part of the in-service program, the administrator's role is
to provide the structure, the means, the content, the motivation, and the leadership to move the staff forward
toward its common goals. In the second part of the in-
service program, the administrator and board provide encouragement, opportunity, and the means for the teacher
to develop his or her individual interests and talents.

Effective programs for staff development have certain
aspects or guidelines which give them substance. Already
mentioned were the assessment of the local needs and the
necessity for the board and administrator to provide the
staff with time, means, and leadership. That, however, is
not enough. The board and administrator must also create a favorable atmosphere, an atmosphere that honors
and encourages initiative, mutual respect, creativeness,
and the freedom to try and even, perhaps, to fail. These
goals simply will not be realized if the teacher feels that
the administrator does not really care whether or not
professional improvement is being pursued.

The improvement program of each teacher will differ
and will include a variety of activities. There will be action activities such as visiting other schools to observe
master teachers, attending workshops and conferences,
and introducing new approaches in the classroom. There
also will be research activities. This research may involve
the actual carrying out of a research project in the classroom, or it may be research into what others have done
or written.

Not only should every teacher be encouraged to write out his or her own self-improvement plan, but that plan should also be reviewed and evaluated periodically with the administrator. This means that a record of activities will be kept. Some schools use a standard form for this purpose. The evaluation need not be an involved procedure. Merely a review of what has been done, what has been undone, and what still should be done can provide the drive needed to keep the program moving in the right direction.

The location and size of the school will affect the opportunities of teachers. Those who are in large-city areas have a wide variety of enrichment opportunities at their fingertips. In other areas the selection is limited and the staff must take advantage of every opportunity provided. Courses, conferences, lectures, extension programs, visiting other schools, institutes, workshops, university programs, teacher exchanges, and travel are some of the inservice opportunities that can be considered part of a teacher's self-improvement program.

In all of this, the board can give its encouragement by providing leaves of absence, summer projects, financial reimbursements, and a salary system which gives recognition to those who make an effort to improve. The board must recognize that a mediocre school can be made a great school by improving its staff. Staff members will not greatly improve unless the board uses various means to encourage them to grow.

Staff improvement can also be fostered by a good inschool in-service program, involving staff planning of faculty meetings which focus on certain self-determined needs. The major items to be considered should be announced well in advance so that staff members can review and prepare for the topic. This gives the staff a stake in the meeting and prevents a situation in which the success of the meeting depends solely on those who present the topic. The most useful faculty meetings reduce the time spent on routine administrative matters, thus affording extra time to be spent on matters involving professional growth.

In larger schools, departmental or grade-level meetings offer opportunity for teacher-to-teacher exchange of ideas, techniques, and methods. A group of smaller schools can arrange for joint service days or half days. On these occasions subject-area or grade-level meetings can be held. The administrator's role is to make the arrangements with other area administrators so that the program will be most beneficial for the staff. Administrators provide the leadership; staff members provide the needed expertise.

The Payoff

Emphasis on teacher in-service programs is no doubt a primary responsibility of the alert Christian-school administrator. In terms of improved education, no other effort will yield better results. Although research into the relationship between in-service training and teacher competency is meager at best, a supportive study was made some years ago in the Los Angeles school system. This study concluded that those teachers who participated extensively in in-service activities displayed an improved relationship with their students; their management of the classroom and academic presentations were more effective. Furthermore, relationships within the school, among school patrons, and with the public in general were strengthened.

Other professions have long recognized the benefits of in-service training. The medical profession generally requires a regular schedule of sessions to update knowledge and skills. It is logical that professionals who work independently from other professionals need to review, test, and improve their performance by communication with others in their field. Such interaction among teaching colleagues not only imparts information and improves skills, but even carries with it a social-professional dimension which benefits the teacher as well as the school and the student. It is perhaps the only practical way that teaching professionals can change and improve.

5

Focusing on the Student

Different groups regard schools in different ways. To the nation, schools are training grounds where people will learn to rule themselves well. To the community, the school is the place where the future work force and concerned citizens are trained. To the church, the school—the *Christian* school—is the source of a knowledgeable membership that can successfully do God's work among men. To the family and parent, the Christian school is the right-hand helper in providing Christian direction to children. To the board, the Christian school is a heavy responsibility because providing a Christian education for our children is required by the God who invited little children to come to Him. To the teachers and staff members, the Christian school is a place of service to God and man, as well as a source of livelihood. To the child, the school contains all the hopes and fears of the future. It is a training ground which will have a profound effect on what the child's life ultimately will be. It is the child who has by far the largest stake in the school.

Today some schools seem to have lost sight of their primary task. The major portion of the literature concerned with schools seems to concern itself with the means of education. Comparatively little seems to be written concerning the primary focus of schools, the child. School board and staff meetings are consumed by issues mechanical or technical in nature, while matters which have firsthand consequence for children often are merely a footnote. It makes one wonder, sometimes, whether some schools have not merely become a place where adults play life's little games and the child is little more than a spectator seated on the bench.

The administrator must not become so bogged down in the techniques of running a school that he or she loses sight of the primary responsibility, the child. The administrator must insure that the school program is in tune with the child's needs and expectations. When staff members worry about what subjects they will teach, who and how many will be in their classes, and a multitude of other details, the administrator must call them back to focus on the child's needs. The instructional program must fit the needs of many different children first of all, and the staff must position its needs within the context of the children's needs.

Each child must be treated as the individual he or she is. This means that each child must have equal access to a challenging and suitable curriculum. Alternative programs should be provided where the uniqueness of a child calls for such an approach. The student is to be regarded as a person, as an individual. This means that the child's privacy and personal rights are safeguarded. It also means that the child's voice is at least sought and listened to. Actions which deprive a student of any measure of participation in determining the learning process must be weighed in the light of adult standards of justice.

It is not enough to treat children kindly and as persons in their own right. Policies must be adopted which recognize the vulnerability of children. Measures must be taken which give the child a safe, secure, and healthy environment. This means that administrators must be protective of the children, keeping them from the dangers they face on all fronts. The school has a vital interest in the child, if not a legal responsibility for him or her while in as well as on the way to and from school. Safety precautions must be taken so the child will always arrive at school and at home safely. Reasonable precautions must also be taken at school to protect the child from the actions of other students and from the health hazards that the school environment may hold for children.

A Matter of Discipline

Concern for the student means that a certain discipline must exist in the school. The person ultimately responsible for maintaining this discipline is the administrator. The administrator must see to it that rules of behavior are established and that penalties are applied for misconduct. Although in most situations it will be staff members who administer discipline to students, the administrator's influence and authority will be felt. If the administrator falters in resolve to maintain an orderly school, the school will inevitably become disorderly, and some students may possibly be placed at risk.

There are limitations on the disciplinary authority of the administrator. Some of these limits are spelled out by law; some can be seen in the precedents established in court decisions. In this regard, Christian schools generally have more control over student behavior than do public schools. Christian schools can establish rules of behavior which would be risky for public schools to impose. For example, certain dress-code regulations may be contested in court if a public-school administrator seeks to impose them, but can be applied by a Christian-school administrator with little, if any, risk of challenge.

In spite of the fact that the administrator's disciplinary powers have limits, he or she still must establish standards of behavior and see that those standards are enforced in the school. No Christian school can tolerate insubordination, vandalism, use of drugs, stealing, use or possession of weapons, disobedience, cheating, fighting, excessive absenteeism or tardiness, and behavior which in other ways disrupts the school in its purposes. Although students today have a highly developed sense of fairness and of their rights, they do accept discipline when they realize it is necessary to operate an orderly school, when they have something to say about the rules, and when justice is administered equally to everyone.

The standards of behavior expected of children in school are based on a Christian philosophy of discipline. This means that there exists first of all a respect for God's laws. Acceptance of these laws is shown in our dealings with each other; it is evidenced in the courtesy and respect we grant one another, our morality, and attitudes. The limits of acceptable behavior must be clearly defined and fully understood by all. Generally an administrator should be governed by a rule of reasonableness. The question, "What would the parents do in this situation?" should be at least one of the tests of reasonableness. The Christian school still believes in the principle of *in loco parentis* and therefore deals with the child in the way Christian parents would deal with their child. A reasonable standard of courtesy, consideration, and concern is always present in the application of justice and authority.

Much has been written on discipline in the school. Yet a few basic points should be made because they will be useful to administrators, staff members, and board members. What follows is by no means a comprehensive offering on disciplining children, but a few suggestions that have been found useful by others in responsible roles.

Visibility

Isn't it amazing how traffic tends to slow when a police cruiser makes an appearance? There is great deterrent value in visibility. If the administrator remains in the office, students will grow bold and mischief will prevail. The highly successful high-school principal makes it a point to walk the halls and grounds whenever the student body is moving. His or her example and encouragement lead some of the staff to be visible also. The result is a well-ordered school.

The practice of standing in front of the school each morning to greet students not only demonstrates friendliness and concern but also builds confidence in the management of the school. It tends to discourage tardiness, smoking, and loitering outside the building.

The principal can avoid the appearance of being a spy or policeman by greeting and talking to students. This tends to encourage students to stop in when something is wrong, especially if they have ready access to the principal when they do come to the office. Visibility is a big plus!

Efficient Discipline

A student should be allowed to "face the music" as soon as possible. Disciplining a child may not fit neatly into the administrator's busy schedule, but it should be remembered that a sensitive child will be upset if he is detained a long time after making a once-in-a-lifetime misstep. Of course, a cooling-off period may be called for, but such a period should be calculated and planned, not a fixed policy for every discipline case.

The punishment must not only fit the case, but it must be carried out as quickly as possible. Every administrator sooner or later finds a student who will run up such a series of misbehaviors that the imposition of discipline extends into weeks or months. An administrator and teacher must know when to stop piling it on. The burden of retribution can become so great in the student's mind that he or she just becomes more angry and disruptive. The administrator must know when to wipe the slate clean and give someone a fresh start. Efficient discipline is quick, of short duration, to the point, appropriate for the misbehavior, and felt to be just.

A Good Start

Start right, end right. A take-charge administrator who has given much thought, planning, and attention to details will reap big dividends in the smooth running of the school. This is as true for the teacher in the classroom as it is for the administrator in the hallways, on the grounds, and in the office. If children do not sense a strong hand in control, they will probe and see how much rope has been left for them to use; they will take advantage of whatever openings they find.

The wise administrator makes sure that all schedules are ready, all rules known, all procedures understood, all penalties defined, and routines established. The wise administrator or teacher learns the names, faces, and records of students as soon as possible. He or she is friendly but firm and fair, and not too sensitive about being considered strict. Teachers and students should be helped to realize that everyone benefits when each does his or her part to maintain a well-disciplined learning environment.

Self-discipline

Children are like adults in that they often will not do much more than what is required of them. If you tell a worker to produce ten pieces an hour, he is unlikely to produce twenty. If you tell a child no homework is expected, none will be done.

Expectations and self-discipline go hand in hand. If much is expected of the child, he or she will tend to discipline his or her own desires and habits to conform to that expectation. Of course, there is a point of diminishing returns. One must judge what a child is capable of doing without feeling pressures that may be damaging.

School personnel do children a favor when they are required to extend themselves in order to learn. This will give them self-discipline, which in turn will tend to give them the self-assurance they need to accomplish their goals.

Homework challenges children to extend themselves. It must be work that can readily be done without help, it must be appropriate to the child's needs, and it must be useful in fulfilling the requirements of the subject or course. Homework must involve a reasonable amount of time. The time involved must be matched to the age and ability of the child. Homework must be regular so that good study habits will be formed. Hit-or-miss homework is of negative value. It will be resented and will not build self-discipline.

Strict but Fair

Perhaps one of the best compliments students can pay a teacher or administrator is that he or she is strict but fair. Some administrators try too hard to be "Mr. Nice Guy." These people are often viewed by students as having favorites because whoever asks most usually gets most. Objectivity in granting requests is not easy to maintain because some students and teachers have a pleasant way of asking while others are timid or awkward. An administrator who places his or her own popularity above strictness or fairness is courting trouble.

The administrator cannot become just another member of the group and maintain the aura of respect needed to keep control. Surely he or she should be helpful, friendly, and loving, and show respect to students and teachers, but the administrator's role as the person in charge must be understood.

Immediate satisfaction does not necessarily transmit into long-range respect. The balance between friendliness and familiarity is a delicate one, and a sensitive administrator knows just when the balance tips.

Perhaps one of the most difficult tasks is to like everyone. Some children and teachers are easy to like. Some are a constant thorn in the flesh. It is well for Christian administrators to remember that the child who is the hardest to like may be the child who most needs to be liked. The time of greatest danger in these delicate relationships is when one is angry. The administrator who is given to righteous wrath should remember to keep his or her hands at home so they will not later be a cause of regret. When there is the temptation to put one's hands on a student, it is advisable to try to substitute an attitude of love or parentlike affection. The image the administrator projects takes a lot of time to form but can be destroyed in one weak moment. The wise administrator remembers the words *strict*, *fair*, and *loving* when dealing with the lovable and the not-so-lovable.

In Times of Stress

Special situations, such as a public program or a graduation ceremony, can be stressful for those in responsible positions. One wants everything to go smoothly, but some students may view the event as a time to show off or act up. Such events require a special standard of behavior and the wise teacher or administrator makes the special standard well known to students in advance. How the special occasion is handled can reinforce respect or destroy it.

There are places, such as the library, the school bus, and sports events, where special discipline standards must be clearly drawn, clearly understood, and clearly enforced. These standards of behavior must not be overlooked if order is to be maintained.

Manners and Courtesy

A Christian should have good manners and be courteous—this is vital if one is to be Christlike. The administrator must be a model for the staff and children. This means that he or she uses phrases like "please," "thank you," "pardon me," and "excuse me," and expects others to use them as well. A warm greeting and/or farewell are also important.

The wise administrator realizes that the homes from

which children come offer a variety of models—some good, some not so good. Sometimes one must start at the beginning and show consideration of each child whatever his or her present state of manners. It would surely be counterproductive to attempt to teach manners by belittling a child. Manners must be taught in a mannerly way. This means that shaming someone has no place in the school, and criticism is to be used sparingly—if it is used, it is always aimed at the action, not the person.

The more specific one is concerning manners and courtesy, the more likely one is to get results. General, broad attacks on poor manners accomplish very little; on the other hand, requiring that "please" precede each request is a good beginning. Whatever one does, one's expectations of children should be realistic. Children are not adults and should not be expected to act like adults. It is a sad commentary on our times when many children exceed adults in politeness—but do not expect too much too soon.

Chewing Gum and Such

To chew or not to chew, that is the question. I would be so bold as to forbid chewing gum, at least in the classroom, in church, at a funeral, and in the administrator's office. Whatever your position on chewing gum in the school may be, it should at least be consistent. All children in the school should be controlled by the same standard so that all feel equally and fairly treated. This principle applies to all types of discipline and behavior. One teacher should not prove how amiable he or she is by allowing gum-chewing while everyone else is following a different standard. The staff should agree on a policy and all should stick to it.

Here, as in setting other standards of behavior, it is important not to vacillate. Children will accept a standard if it does not shift from day to day. However, it is a good idea to keep gum-chewing and similar issues in the correct context. Gum-chewing students can study and

learn. Because matters like gum-chewing are small problems, they should not become large obstructions to the
tranquility of the school. Good administrators make
mountains out of mountains and molehills out of molehills.

Punishment

"Let the punishment suit the crime." That is good advice for judges, parents, *and school administrators*. The
word *punish* conjures up images of harshness and even
revenge. Jesus taught us that punishment is an inevitable
result of sin. He also taught us that His grace can replace
punishment. The wise administrator balances grace with
punishment by taking measures which teach without creating resentment. Such a balance takes the wisdom of
Solomon and sensitivity of Jesus.

The feelings and attitudes of an administrator are bound
to enter into any exercise of punishment. One must guard
against acting out of anger, revenge, or spite. Punishment
must be the logical conclusion to improper behavior. One
must resist feelings of personal hostility. The age of the
children also should be considered. Can the child com-
prehend the cause-and-effect relationship between misbehavior and punishment? Consider the nature of the
situation and the nature of the child. Does the child really
understand the nature of the misbehavior? Does he or she
know why what happened is inappropriate? What is the
effect of the punishment on other people? Will the punishment place an unreasonable burden on the child, on
the teacher, on the parent, on other children? The punishment must not needlessly affect the innocent.

Students should have a good indication as to the sort
of behavior which will result in punishment and what the
punishment is likely to be. Consistency is a good aid to
prevention. Certainty of punishment is a deterrent. This
means that punishment is not administered in anger, is
not unduly postponed, and is not merely threatened.

Punishment must be aimed at the guilty. It is usually a mistake to punish a whole class no matter how frustrating certain behaviors may be. When the guilty and innocent are punished equally, the class is more likely to turn against the authority figure who administers the unfair punishment than against the guilty student.

Perhaps equally as negative as far as ultimate results is the assignment of schoolwork as punishment. Students can come to associate schoolwork with punishment, and to regard certain types of schoolwork as distasteful. Such a result is self-defeating since the goal of a school is to open horizons and to develop a love for knowledge. Long assignments of writing out words or lines as punishment can result in careless habits of handwriting, inaccuracy, and a lack of pride in one's work.

A word of caution about punishment: one should have a clear understanding of state (or provincial) laws regarding corporal punishment if that is going to be considered. The school board may have some definite ideas about detention or suspension of students. It may also wish to limit the conditions under which corporal punishment can be administered. When it comes to punishing other people's children, more than an ounce of precaution is advisable. A clear understanding before the fact may save much heartache after the fact.

All parents know how difficult it is to administer punishment to their children. It is difficult to be judge, jury, and executor in cases of misbehavior. Remember, the one little incident may soon be forgotten but a misapplied punishment may be remembered for a lifetime. Teachers should be remembered as teachers and administrators as administrators—not as tyrants.

The key to properly applied punishment is love. The child should first understand why punishment is being administered. Then it should be administered in love.

The Parental Role

"I'll tell your parents" should not be used as an idle threat when Jim or Sue presents a continuing problem in the classroom or in the school. For the child's welfare, the administrator and the teacher must consult with the parent. Often parent and teacher together can accomplish for the child what neither is able to accomplish alone. The extra time that an after-school or evening conference may take is often well worth the added effort—and it will express the administrator's and teacher's concern to the parent better than words could ever do.

The conference will be more worthwhile if information on the child has been gathered. The administration should talk to his or her former teachers as well as the present one, look at the child's work and records, and confer with other staff members who might be able to contribute helpful information.

It is difficult for parents to come to school to talk to the administrator or teacher, so they should be set at ease. A warm and friendly greeting and a genuine concern about their child will form a basis for understanding. Avoid implying any blame for the child's conduct. Rather, seek information and confer about the common interest all of you have in the child. The key question you will want to ask is, "What can we do to improve the situation?" Seek their suggestions—and have some ready for them, too.

The child can benefit from the knowledge that administrator, teacher, and parents have a common concern for his or her well-being. You may wish to discuss the conference with the child afterwards, especially if you have learned something which helped you to better understand his or her problem. At times it may be well to have the child attend part of the conference. But be careful if you do. You will not want the parents to use the occasion to impress on you how strict they are with the child by turning on the child in your presence. Such a situation may result in more resentment and more difficulty with the child later.

Once contact with the parents has been established, be sure to keep this channel open. Call or write occasionally to let the parents know how their child is getting along. Have a follow-up conference to report how suggestions made at the first conference are working out. Keep records of the conferences and any other useful information, because such information may be helpful at a later time—to the parents, the child, and future teachers.

The parent and teacher must recognize that the purpose of the conference is to foster positive behavior. One avenue that should not be overlooked is praise. It does not help to praise a child when he or she knows praise is not deserved. Praise has a powerful influence on children, but it must be honestly given. That does not mean that you should not look long and hard for some praiseworthy action—you should. All children have some talents, special attributes, or positive accomplishments. The key is to be appreciative of small things. Just to notice a smile may be enough for one child. "You have a nice smile today" may have within it more positive motivation than "That was a great no-hit game you pitched."

It is a good exercise for all of us to seek the praiseworthy, positive things in others. Too often we notice defects. We would all improve our Christian image if only we trained ourselves to appreciate the good points in others. A teacher who notes the positive points will have fewer problem children.

Do not overdo praise, however. Overpraising can be as deadening as can underpraising. A lot of gushy words soon fall on deaf ears. Vary the form of your praise: a smile, a motion, or a single word can sometimes do wonders for a child who is not sure if he or she is even noticed.

The administrator can be a shining example for others to follow. Usually the school reflects that example. If the administrator is an appreciative person, others will follow, and the atmosphere of the school will be positive.

Respect for Others

Respect for others is one Christian virtue greatly needed today. Children learn respect for others, at least partially, by being shown respect. Belittling, shaming, or embarrassing a student may get some immediate results that seem to fill the bill at the time, but in the process the child is learning a lesson which may have injurious effects on the way he or she treats others. These short-term gains are too costly in the long run and are not worthy of Christian leaders.

There are vast differences among people. Recognition of differences in religion, nationality, race, and personal or physical characteristics, forms an excellent starting point for lessons in respect. That is why a Christian school is fortunate when it has a variety of religious backgrounds, races, and personalities. In such a school a child can learn to respect people for who they are, not for what they look like or what they presently believe. It is essential for children to learn what to value in a person. Today, appearance and personality seem to be the keys to acceptance and future financial success. Christian children should learn instead to value the characteristics that Christ taught are important, namely, love of God and love of each other.

The Christian-school classroom must help children to face their prejudices and to correct them. It must help them temper feelings of hostility toward those whom they have come to regard as enemies. It must condition them not to classify people according to race or national origins. All of this must be done in a context where all children are regarded and treated equally, where all are given the same fair treatment.

Teachers and administrators must be alert to their own

attitudes and guard against those little signals of bias that children are especially quick to imitate. For example, watch the traps inherent in the use of nicknames. Watch the way students are grouped, and the way they are addressed, shown affection, or reprimanded. Think twice and then think again when tempted to prejudge because of "his parents," "his church," "his weight," "his race," or "his ability." Prejudice may be rampant in today's world but the Christian-school administrator must fight mightily to keep it out of the Christian school.

Environment

An elderly colleague once suggested that what students wear and their surroundings will surely make a big difference in their behavior. Pointing to three boys who were wearing their Sunday best and walking like gentlemen, he said, "They would be walking on walls and jumping fences if they had on their blue jeans."

That is true. Dress does influence behavior. Of course, today's jeans are no longer considered suitable only for work. We are in the age of "dress" jeans. Nonetheless, attire does affect behavior and a school must consider what, if any, limits it should place on attire.

The appearance and environment of the classroom and school are as important as dress. An unkempt school can mean more careless students, students less concerned about neat and careful work. ("Neat and careful" obviously isn't all that important; just look at the school and the classroom.) Of course, that attitude can be reversed. A well-kept environment can encourage students to be neat and careful in their work.

The administrator should make a regular tour of the school with an eye toward the environment in which the children and staff must live and work. Look at the walls. Are the bulletin boards current and lively? Do they teach? Look at the flat surfaces. Are they cluttered and untidy?

Are unattractive items kept in cabinets and closets, or are they out in the open, adding a bit of ugliness? What about the cupboards and closets? Are they orderly and neat? Some students like the task of cleaning drawers or closets. Ask them to help; it will give them a stake in the appearance of their school.

The halls, the school office, and the grounds should also be viewed with a critical eye. Is it really necessary for the box of balls and bats to be in the main hallway? When was the hallway floor last waxed? Isn't there a better place to store the gym mats? Don't forget the outside appearance—the grass and the weeds, the flowers and the trees.

If the administrator and staff show pride in the school by keeping it attractive and pleasant, they will find the students sharing that pride and concern. Student behavior can be improved by positive physical surroundings. Use your school and classrooms to help, not hinder, in your effort to have a well-disciplined school.

6

Designing Educational Programs

The administrator of a school has the responsibility to allocate its resources in a way which gives maximum benefit to the children. This means that certain decisions must be made concerning the educational program of the school. There must be immediate and long-term curriculum objectives.

The Christian school's curriculum and practices must be consistent with its goals and principles. That statement may seem obvious and simple, but the situation is most complex. No administrator can hope to design a finely-tuned educational program by himself. The involvement of staff, an educational committee, and outside consultants is needed. The complexities of the undertaking mean the administrator must rely on outside help to do the job adequately. Years ago, Christian Schools International recognized the need schools have for curriculum planning. This recognition motivated CSI to spend much of its efforts in the area of curriculum development. The Christian-school administrator would do well to use the materials and services which CSI offers in curriculum development.

The purpose of this book is not to review the philo-

79

sophical underpinnings of a Christian-school curriculum. Other writers have done that well. Nicholas Wolterstorff's *Curriculum: By What Standard?* and Henry Beversluis's *Christian Philosophy of Education* will give a Christian-school administrator the necessary basic insights into Christian-school philosophy. CSI has also published materials which help schools make the transition from basic philosophy to classroom application. Wolterstorff's *Education for Responsible Action: Goals for Christian Education* (a companion discussion guide is also available) and *Principles to Practice* by Henry Triezenberg and others give enough background to develop a meaningful Christian-school curriculum. CSI is presently in the process of producing a *Curriculum Writer's Handbook*.

All of this is to assure the school administrator that he or she need not attempt to do it alone. Curriculum planning is an enormous responsibility that cannot be ignored, but help is at hand.

One of the primary tasks of the school administrator is to provide leadership in the areas of curriculum organization and instructional improvement. The manner in which this is done will be strongly influenced by the administrator's concept of a good Christian-school program. One of the basic issues concerns the type of grade organization of the school. Is a K-8-4, 4-4-4, 6-3-3, K-6-3-3, or K-9-3 arrangement best suited for your school program? Christian-school educators have long debated the place and role of kindergarten. Now these same concerns are being expressed about preschool programs. Other Christian-school leaders have debated the place of ninth grade. Does it belong with the middle school or with the high school? The response to these and a number of other questions predisposes a certain type of educational program.

Grade arrangement is just one of many basic questions which the administrator seeks to help answer for his constituency. Most established schools do not debate that issue any longer; they live with the grade arrangement presently in existence.

Schools must, however, seek the answer to other organizational problems. A basic question concerns the school curriculum—what is it, or what should it be? What should the school teach, and to what extent? At one time the school curriculum was thought of as a series of courses, but today we have come to think of it more as a series of growing or learning experiences provided for the children. These growing or learning experiences must be planned. They must be sequential, and within the range of the child's ability to learn. They must reflect the principles which we hold and which we wish our children to acquire. They must be complete and comprehensive enough so as not to allow any gaps which would render the program incomplete and possibly inadequate.

Competent educators often disagree about what should be included in the educational experience of the child. Some educators believe in "hands on" learning, in experience, in learning by doing, in firsthand absorption. Others believe in a reasoning experience of the mind, as obtained by the use of books and similar learning materials. Some like a combination of these two approaches which focuses on solving problems within the child's experiences.

What or who should determine the direction of a school? The administrator must guide parents and staff in refining opinions and determining directions for the school. This is no small task because it involves defining the issues, debating their merits, making sure that the issues are understood and, finally, making decisions.

The administrator must also guide parents and staff in determining which demands the program will seek to fulfill. Obviously, there are basic demands on every child to obtain a functional level of basic competency. These are sometimes referred to as reading, writing, and arithmetic. These basics are needed by everyone. Beyond these basic demands are the demands of parents who have high goals for their children. Then there are the goals of the church, which wants its people to be prepared for every good work, and the demands of society, in which each of us must function as a part of a larger whole. There is the demand of the state that a person become a responsible citizen. There is the demand of God that a child become His light and His salt. Someone must sort out these demands, give them a priority ranking, and cast them into an educational program. Everyone in the Christian-school community has a responsibility for the program, but it is the school administrator who has a unique leadership role. His or her structuring, organizing, and motivating are essential to clarity of direction and purpose in the school program.

One does not offer education to a child as one would offer an assortment of candy bars. It is not just a matter of feeding a child in accordance with his or her desires or the desires of the teachers. Children vary, and a teaching diet suitable for one child may be too rich for another child. This presents another learning situation that the staff must solve. How does a school and, particularly, how does a classroom adjust to individual differences? This is one of the primary problems facing a classroom teacher, and an area where administrative leadership must be applied.

One need not work with children long to discover that their learning rates vary. (Of course, learning expectations can influence the degree to which ability is put to work.) Therefore, one course of study given to all at a pre-ordained rate will bore some and completely lose others. Some teachers have sought to solve the problems created by individual differences by grouping children according to their abilities. This works better with some learning tasks than with others. A drawback is that children soon realize which group is the slow group.

Some teachers have sought to solve the difficulty by

using a problem-centered, experience-type curriculum which permits the group to work together on a common problem. Each class member contributes to the solution of the problem at his or her level of development.

Some teachers have devised a learning situation involving individualized programs. Each child "contracts" with the teacher every day to do certain tasks which are within the child's ability range. Classrooms using such programs usually consist of a variety of learning centers where children obtain the materials and information needed to carry out the terms of their "contract."

One soon recognizes that the learning program of a school involves both content and process. These two aspects of a school program are inseparably related. Both must be worked out by the school leadership in a way that meets the needs of the student, the goals of the parents, the objectives of the Christian community, and the purposes of the state. Success in these efforts depend in large measure on how well Christian school leaders are able to manage the elements of the curriculum.

7

Managing School Finances

Christian-school leaders may have high expectations and goals for their school, but the actual realization of those goals will depend to a great extent on the financial support the school receives. Christian schools are financed in four primary ways: the parents usually pay a tuition, supporting churches contribute by taking offerings or by establishing a support quota, individuals contribute as a result of solicitation (usually during fund-raising campaigns), and, as in some Canadian provinces, the government offers grants to the schools.

The administrator of the school is responsible to see that the needed funding is received. This process is an educational one first of all. People must know why they should support Christian schools; it is the school's task to educate the people on this matter. In the process, certain principles, including biblical principles, must be communicated. There is the principle of individual responsibility. God has given children to parents and with that gift comes the responsibility to educate those children in His ways. It is incumbent upon the parents, to the best of their ability, to provide for the Christian education of their children. There is also the principle of corporate responsibility. Christians not only have a responsibility for their own children, but they also have a responsibility for each other's children. I Corinthians 12 describes the church as a body whose members need each other. Galatians 6:2 calls on the members of the body of believers to "bear one another's burdens, and so fulfill the law of Christ." The Bible calls on us to show our love to God by showing our love to each other. One way to express this love is to share each other's financial burdens by providing a Christian education for all children of the Christian family.

We are not all equally blessed financially, and so there is a need for some to give more than others, according to their blessings. This is the principle of proportionate giving. The Old Testament law of a 10 percent tithe was an indication of this principle. In the New Testament the principle of proportionate giving was extended. Jesus recognized that the widow who gave two coins had given more than others who may have offered much larger contributions, but a far smaller percentage of their income. In I Corinthians 16:2 Paul encouraged everyone to give as God had prospered him.

These biblical principles lead to other principles which many Christian schools have adopted. Many Christian schools have an understanding that no child should be deprived of a Christian education because of the financial inability of parents to pay for that education. They also believe in the responsibility of the entire Christian community for the Christian education of all of its children. They recognize the individual's responsibility to determine his or her own personal obligation to the school in the light of God's blessings. A financial plan, whatever it may be, is not the solution to meeting a school's financial needs. Rather, the solution rests in the generous hearts of the school's supporters. The school leadership can and must provide the constituents with information and guidelines to assist them in determining what is a proper commitment for them to make in the light of the needs of the school and their own fiscal situation.

Tuition Plans

There are various tuition plans that are being or have been used by Christian schools:

1. Some schools have a single tuition rate which fully covers the cost of education. In effect, the school divides its budget by the number of students, and arrives at the cost per pupil. This figure becomes the tuition. Such an approach does not take into account the biblical principle of corporate responsibility and is used by only a few schools.
2. Some schools calculate the total cost of education but establish a tuition rate which is only a percentage of that total cost. If through experience a school finds that 20 percent of its funds can be raised by gifts, it uses an 80-20 formula, the tuition is set at 80 percent of the cost per pupil.
3. Instead of a single tuition rate, some schools use a sliding scale, which means that the rate for two children is less than double the rate for one child, and the proportionate rate per child for a family of three children is less than that for a family of two children. The idea here is that larger families should have their tuition bill moderated.
4. Some schools carry the sliding scale to its logical end and establish a "family" tuition. This is a single tuition rate for every family regardless of how many children attend school. This recognizes that the financial burden on a family usually increases as the number of children in the family increases. Some parents with only one child in school may object to this arrangement because they are required to pay more than the educational cost for their child.
5. Variable or negotiated tuition is used by some schools in an effort to more accurately consider the financial circumstances of each family. In a negotiated-tuition

program, a school official discusses the school's financial needs with the parent in an effort to assist the parent in making a reasonable financial commitment to the school. Usually guidelines, such as a "share-giving guide," are provided the parent to assist in a reasonable determination. The share-giving guide suggests payments in accordance with income levels. The figures in the guide are predicated at levels which will furnish the financial needs of the school. Here, too, the funds to be provided by parents may have to be only 70 or 80 percent of the total need, for nonparents may meet the other 20 to 30 percent of the need. The compilation of a reasonable share-giving guide will involve much research into the income levels of the constituency, the average number of children per family, and the number and generosity of nonparent supporters.

6. Some schools have substituted for a share-giving guide what is called a percentage-giving plan. They determine what percentage of the average income is needed from parent and nonparent in order to support the school. A typical plan may determine that 2 percent of the income of everyone in the school community is needed. Parents are asked to contribute additional amounts equal to 5 percent of income for one child, 7.5 percent of income for two children, and 9 percent of income for three or more children. These percentages will of course vary with the individual school.

In some Christian-school communities another financial need is being met. There are Christian parents, particularly in the inner cities, who desire a Christian education for their children but cannot afford to pay tuition. In Grand Rapids, Michigan, for example, the Evangelical Committee for Christian Education Scholarships (ECCES) seeks to raise funds for some of these children.

In past years, up to fifty students have been helped. This committee, which is supported by contributions, carefully screens all applications for assistance.

The Rochester (New York) Christian School has a Tuition Aid Fund which it uses for the benefit of inner-city children. The Calvin Christian School Association of Wyoming, Michigan, has a Grant Assistance Plan which it uses to assist needy students. The Evangelical Committee for Urban Ministries in Paterson (ECUMP), an arm of the Eastern Christian School Association, provides scholarships for inner-city children. These are just a few of the schools which have recognized the need and have established funds to help meet it.

In providing a program for Christian stewardship, some Christian schools have assisted constituents to contribute from their estates both before and after death. They offer advice in estate planning. This advice can result in tax benefits to individuals and in long-term giving for worthy causes. The will is a basic instrument for all good stewards of God's gifts. Wise planning can insure that a large part of a person's estate will go to the causes he or she chooses to support. While a will is a short-term instrument to dispose of property after death, a trust extends over a period of years; in a sense, it can be described as a long-term will.

A trust is an arrangement by which a certain amount of property is set aside to be managed by another person for one or more beneficiaries. A person can stipulate in a trust just how the property is to be managed and who will receive its income. Through a trust a person can control the estate for as long as twenty-one years after the last person designated in the trust dies. There are basically two types of trusts: the testamentary trust, which becomes effective at death, and the *inter vivos* or living trust, which can be created during life and continued after death.

In addition to wills and trusts, both of which can have

tax benefits if they are carefully planned, some schools provide an annuity plan for their constituents. In such a plan, a person makes a substantial gift to a Christian school and receives from the school a guaranteed fixed annual income for the rest of his or her life. Advantages of the annuity are that part of it is deductible from taxable income and a large percentage of each interest payment is exempt from federal income tax. In addition, by taking money out of an estate, one can eliminate future probate costs and estate taxes. Thus estate-planning services are often of great benefit to the constituent while they offer a means of support for Christian schools. Estate planning can offer peace of mind, tax savings, and financial assistance for worthy institutions.

Financial Campaigns

A means of financial support used often enough to warrant special mention is the fund-raising campaign. Many Christian schools have occasional or annual fund-raising campaigns.

Fund-raising campaigns are conducted for two main purposes: to supplement the general operating funds of the school and to provide funds for new buildings or other capital needs. Today the drive to supplement general funds is not as common as it once was. But when a school finds it needs to build a gym or more classrooms, it will usually conduct a financial campaign to raise the funds. Christian Schools International offers some basic advice on how to conduct a financial campaign. The mechanics of a successful campaign are not complicated. Usually success depends on the enthusiasm of those who help with the campaign.

There are a few matters that should be kept in mind if a financial campaign is to be a success:

1. There must be a clearly evident need for funds, and this need must be communicated in a convincing way.
2. The leadership, especially the drive chairman, must be carefully selected for ability and for enthusiasm.
3. One cannot overdo publicity for the drive. The best person available should be charged with getting the message to the people. This requires both someone with communication skills and an adequate budget to fully use those skills. Remember to use a many-faceted approach. The more variety in your communication, the more likely it is that everyone will get the message.
4. In addition to good leadership and good communication, one needs good organization. This involves appointing a capable organizational chairman and energetic captains who recruit eager workers. Everyone is given a manageable task with a precise timetable. Activities are not allowed to be delayed but are continuously being enthusiastically pursued. If a worker does not report at the designated time, he or she is immediately called and asked to make a firm commitment to a new deadline. Follow-up is not neglected but pursued to the very smallest detail.
5. There should be a kickoff meeting for the drive workers. If the drive is to be successful, that meeting must communicate the need, the goal, and inspiration.
6. There should be an evaluation meeting after the drive. Each detail should be reviewed so that if mistakes were made, they will not be repeated.

The Tax Picture

Today the separation of church and state is frequently debated, but there is one area where Christian schools and the state apparently cannot be separated: that of income taxes and tax deductions. Conflicts and disagreements between tax-collecting agencies and nonpublic schools have existed for years. The tax picture in the United States and Canada is quite similar. Tuition is not tax-deductible in either country, but gifts to Christian schools are tax-deductible. The pertinent question always revolves around the definition of tuition and contributions. In Canada, the issue is further complicated by an effort of Revenue Canada to separate education into religious and secular components, the contention being that support for religious education is tax-exempt, but support for secular education is not.

Of course, most members of Christian Schools International in both the United States and Canada contend that all of life—hence, all of education—is God's and therefore cannot be divided along religious and secular lines. Those school boards that unalterably cling to this position find themselves without tax exemptions for any portion of their children's education. Other boards, while clinging to the concept that all of life is religious, recognize that, as far as the state is concerned, Christian education does fulfill a secular function. Inasmuch as Christian education serves the state's secular educational goals, it is deserving of a tax deduction. This reasoning parallels that which is used to uphold the tax-exempt status of a church. The church does not deserve a tax exemption because of its religious teaching; in fact, the state has no part or portion in the church's philosophy. The state does, however, recognize the positive effect the church has on fostering a good, honest, and loyal citizenry. It also recognizes the church's benevolent activities which benefit the citizenry and, to an extent, relieve the state of some of its obligations. These secular benefits persuade the state to grant tax-exempt status to the church.

One could contend, as indeed some do, that the religious life and the secular functions of the church are inseparable, and indeed they are. Yet the state has determined to separate them because it cannot support a religious teaching but it can support a secular effect by granting a tax benefit.

In the United States, the Internal Revenue Service has not defined the problem in quite the same way as has Revenue Canada, but the effect is similar. The Internal Revenue Service simply points to the law which states that payment for educational services, usually called tuition, is not deductible. It further contends that it does not matter whether that payment is made to the school, to the church, or to some other third party. If it is payment for educational services received, it is not deductible.

There is one exception to that blanket rule. When the church and school are one, that is, when the church and school have a single governing board, and when the school is supported exclusively by church funds, then the school is considered to be a church activity. As such its funds are church funds; and of course, gifts to churches are tax-exempt. However, if the church charges tuition, the tuition is not tax-exempt.

The Internal Revenue Service has used a number of interpretations in its effort to define tuition. One formula widely used holds that all costs are to be considered in defining tuition, with the exception of capital costs, which are characteristically spread over a number of years. In addition, a school may usually deduct from its annual cost figure the gifts received from nonparents. For example, a school receiving 20 percent of its support from nonparents may subtract that portion of the budget and any capital funds prior to calculating the parent's annual cost or tuition figure.

These calculations are made necessary because the Internal Revenue Service will not allow each school simply to set a low tuition rate and conclude that all amounts given beyond that rate are gifts and, hence, tax-exempt. One can see the temptation to establish the lowest possible tuition rate in order to gain greater tax deductibility for parents. Tuition is no longer considered by the Internal

Revenue Service to be just an arbitrary amount determined by a school board. In this contention the tax courts have repeatedly upheld the Internal Revenue Service.

Some Canadian provinces have not felt the full weight of Revenue Canada's policies. Schools in these provinces receive significant per-pupil grants which do tend to relieve their financial burden. Christian schools in British Columbia, Manitoba, and Alberta have significantly benefited from these grants. On the other hand, Christian schools in Ontario find themselves in much the same position as do their counterparts in the United States.

Budget Formulation and Control

The Christian-school administrator is not only concerned about funds received in support of the school but must also concern himself with the control of expenditures. This implies that the administrator sees to it that the budget is carefully formulated and controlled. Various factors should be kept in mind in budget formulation:

1. Budget planning is a continuing year-round responsibility; therefore, the persons involved should be carefully selected, and the tasks for which each is responsible should be clearly delineated.
2. A budget calendar must be formulated and followed.
3. All who are involved in using school funds should be consulted when the budget is formulated. This means staff members should be consulted concerning expenditures for classrooms and for educational material, the custodian concerning janitorial supplies, the school secretary concerning office supplies, and the pertinent board committees concerning their responsibilities.
4. Budget worksheets, along with summaries of past budgets and expenditures, should be supplied to all involved.

5. One person should be designated to gather all the information to be used in formulating a tentative budget proposal.
6. The tentative budget should be reviewed by all those who have made some suggestions for it.
7. The finance committee should refine the tentative budget for presentation to the entire school board.
8. The school board then reviews, refines, changes where necessary, and finally approves the budget.
9. The budget is then submitted to the full association or society for approval.

The expenditure of budget funds is best controlled by good monthly reporting to the board. There was a time when boards approved every bill for payment. Fortunately, such time-consuming and unnecessary board activity has been given over to the school treasurer and the administrator in most schools. Some larger school systems rely completely upon the superintendent and/or the business manager. Some school boards still retain the prerogative of approving bills above a certain amount. Most boards consider a monthly review as an adequate check on school expenditures.

In such monthly checks, funds that seem to be overspent are red-lined so that the board can investigate why expenditures seem high. Those funds that need more stringent control are watched, and people who expend from these budget areas are cautioned about the fund's condition.

One must remember, however, that the budget is a means to an end. It is the instrument used to keep track of the level of expenditures. The budget is not an end in itself and need not become the master of school operation. Sometimes important needs are neglected because there is "nothing in the budget." Sometimes, exceeding the budget or transferring funds within the budget is justifiable.

Of course, one cannot continue to overspend the budget or an inevitable day of reckoning will come.

It is the administrator's responsibility to recommend a school program and the items needed to carry it out. It is the board's responsibility to approve the school program and then to budget that which is necessary to carry it out. Some administrators regard the financial problems as beyond their range of responsibility, but educational programs and financial means are so closely related that both fall in the purview of administrative responsibility. There will likely be board members who are more at home with financial matters because of business experiences. The administrator does well to lean heavily on these people.

The Christian school has many facets and needs a wide range of abilities from its leaders if it is going to function well. The area of fund-raising itself requires many different talents. The way these talents are used often spells the difference between a successful school and one that merely operates.

8

Timesavers

With respect to time, are you the captain of the ship or merely a passenger?

Some administrators and teachers are not always able to control events which affect their schedules. These events are like storms at sea and must be dealt with when they occur, but a large part of the day can be managed. All administrators categorize their time—some do so with forethought, others do not. To use time well, one must have a plan.

Monday morning is a good time to plan the week. Compile a list of things which must be done and a list of things you would like to do if time permits. Then arrange that list in order of priority. By Friday afternoon, check the list to see how you fared for the week. No doubt, there will be plenty left over for the new list on Monday.

Perhaps classifying tasks will improve your batting average. Categorize tasks in terms of importance. Some tasks will be top priority. Others will be less important, tasks you really must do—eventually. The least important tasks are those which only you will notice if they remain undone.

The beginning administrator would do well to write down the tasks. The old hand may just mentally assemble them, yet must be disciplined enough to conduct a regular inventory of them. Remember, task management is the antibiotic of procrastination. What gets priority when it comes to your time? Suppose there is a teacher problem, a student problem, and a parent problem. Have you determined which should be tackled first? Such decisions are the raw material which determine the mettle of the administrator. Selection of which task to perform first can determine the degree of success and, to an extent, the degree of stress one has in administering a school.

Levels of Accountability

In determining the selection of a task, one must be mindful of at least five levels of accountability. As Christians, we recognize we are first of all accountable to God. That in itself places a heavy burden on us.

We are also accountable to self. When God reminded us to love our neighbors as ourselves, He was saying that we are accountable to ourselves. "All work and no play makes Jack a dull boy." No administrator worth his salt becomes a dull boy. So within your priorities, give some time to yourself.

We are accountable to our families. One of the greatest regrets of my life is the time that Christian-school administration often made me steal from my family. Give a high priority to time for your family, so you won't regret that your children seldom see you relaxed. Do not cheat them, but do not cheat yourself either. The amazing thing about such deprivation is that no one other than the family and you will know about it or really seem to care about it.

Here we are at the fourth level of accountability and still have not mentioned any accountability to the school. Some administrators give the impression that their school and their job are the number-one priority in their lives. They are wrong, and we should feel sorry for them if that is the case. Nonetheless, there is an accountability to the parents and children you serve. Indeed, the way you serve parents and children will determine to a great extent how well you serve God. If you fail one child, you will be held accountable no doubt by the parent of that child, by that child, *and by your God*. This is the greatest burden of administration and of teaching.

Of course, the administrator also has an accountability to teachers and board members. We sometimes get the impression that for many administrators, teachers and board members are their first concern. They say, "If I don't succeed with the teachers and board members, I don't succeed, period." There is some truth in that if you are talking about survival, but it is a different story if you're talking about accountability. You cannot alienate teachers if you want a happy place to work. And you cannot alienate the board if you want any place at all. But accountability to your teachers and board is number five on your list—a very important number five, but number five nonetheless.

Kinds of Accountability

While there are five *levels* of accountability, there are three *kinds* of accountability. The first is the kind of accountability built into the situation into which you are born. You suddenly find yourself in the world, in a certain place, with a certain set of circumstances. You did not ask to be born, but here you are and within that setting you have acquired a special accountability.

Another kind of accountability is that which you accept from others. When you join a school or club or church, you in essence agree to play according to a set of rules. This may include taking orders from others—or giving orders to them. It may mean living by different agendas and schedules. It may mean a sharing in the lives, the goals, the expectations of others. If you want to remain in good standing in the group, you must recognize a certain accountability to them.

The third kind of accountability is a *shared* experience

which has to do with the interplay of the society in which you live—the organization or order of things. Order is best maintained when a superior shares his accountability with others. Goals are set together and the achievement of the goals is the responsibility of all. Not only does the wise administrator share responsibilities and hold others accountable, but his coworkers are invited to hold him or her accountable for certain goals.

Your situation, your obligation to others, and your ability to share responsibility will, to a great degree, determine how well you use your time. Administrators have developed an entire array of measures to help them better schedule their time. Time-use inventories are used by some. Time-planning sessions with staff and board members are used by others. Planning forms, checklists, and the like have been tried. Some of these measures may be very helpful, and work well for certain people.

You may not know what will work best for you, but if you are going to be happy in your work, you must manage your time well. To do that, you must conscientiously plan your time use. How you do it depends on your style—but do it for the sake of yourself, your family, and your school.

Practical Ideas on Saving Time

The remainder of this chapter consists of a series of hints on how the busy administrator can save time for important tasks.

Handling Mail

Reading and writing letters can be a time-consuming task. One can take a number of steps to do this more effectively:

Learn to read faster. Use different reading techniques for different types of material: scanning, speed-reading, study, analysis.

If you have a secretary, have her underscore the main points of letters and attach previous correspondence and other relevant material. Have your secretary place important mail on top. This means you are going to have to train her to know what is important to you. Allow a set period of time for reading mail. In many cases you may never get to the bottom, and all of the junk mail will end up in the circular file.

Handle mail once. Don't shuffle paper! Take some immediate action. That action might be to pass a letter on to someone else, to answer it, or to scribble some note that will bring it back to you at some future date for action at a more appropriate time. Or immediate action might mean the letter goes into the wastepaper basket. Do not be guilty of sorting things into piles which then get sorted into other piles which eventually end up in still other piles.

Do not dictate letters to your secretary. That takes both your time and hers. Use a recording machine. You might like to write out important letters so you can edit as you go along.

Indicate your response by jotting down notes on the letter. A good secretary often can put your ideas into suitable sentences.

Keep letters as short as possible. Do your debating, with yourself or the addressee, by some more appropriate means. Let your letters document agreements reached.

Handle correspondence by telephone if possible. Letters are expensive! The estimated cost of one page of correspondence (including labor) is from $7.50 to $10.00.

If you do not have a secretary, learn to type. Responding to mail by hand can be extremely time-consuming. Consider using some of the multicopy standard memo forms that offer enough space for a quick reply. This has the advantage of giving you copies of your correspondence without having to deal with carbon paper or copy machines.

Throw away what you will never read. Retain in your files only what you may someday use, and even dispose of that when your goals change. Develop standard replies for questions that arise repeatedly. Put them on 5 by 7 cards, code them, and use them when drafting replies.

Sometimes you will be able to write your reply on the letter you received and send it back. If you wish a record of your reply, make a photocopy of it.

Handling Meetings

Most of us spend more time in meetings than we think we should. Too much time spent in meetings is probably an indication of not enough work being done. Too many meetings are just poorly planned. They are the result of someone's casual "let's get together and talk about it" approach. Meetings do have a unique role to play in accomplishing objectives. There are several legitimate reasons for holding meetings: to create a proper environment in which to address the task at hand, to discuss information rapidly, to develop consensus for a given approach, and, when decisions have been reached, to share responsibility no individual could or should be expected to bear alone.

There are a few basic steps to keep in mind if the meeting is to be successful:

Have a goal for the meeting—both long-range and short-range. What is the purpose of the meeting? What is it you hope to accomplish? If you cannot come up with a purpose, there should be no meeting.

Invite the right people. Who is really needed at the meeting? Avoid inviting people just because you do not want to hurt their feelings. Send them a copy of the minutes, take them out to lunch, or do whatever is needed to show them their not being invited is not an indication of disapproval.

Prepare an agenda with a time schedule on it. If possible, pass out the agenda ahead of time with a statement of purpose written across the top. Use the statement to manage the meeting toward its *purpose*, not toward completing the agenda as planned.

Provide enough time for the meeting. Make sure all decks are cleared so that the necessary time is available.

Be prepared yourself. If you are the leader of the meeting, figure out who should be heard and what role you are going to play.

Start on time—regardless!

Make sure everyone understands the type of meeting you are having. There are basically three kinds of meetings: meetings to announce something already decided, meetings to obtain consensus for something which you have already agreed to do, and meetings to solve a problem or gather ideas. A great deal of confusion and time-wasting occurs when people do not understand what kind of a meeting they are in. A person who thinks the meeting has been called to solve a problem when it actually has been called for the purpose of making an announcement can waste all kinds of time.

Take into account the needs of the participants in the meeting. Meetings of long-established groups and meetings of people put together on an ad hoc basis are quite different. In the former case the participants have worked with each other and have been with each other over a long period of time, but in the latter the participants may know little of each other. If necessary, have the participants get to know each other early in the meeting.

Sum up near the end of the meeting so that it will not ramble to a close.

Announce the results at the end of the meeting, noting, if necessary, what items should be taken up at the next meeting.

End your meeting on time—regardless! A second meeting can be scheduled.

By the way, if you are invited to a meeting at which you are not needed, do not go! Tell the appropriate people your views and let them carry the ball. They will be impressed by your self-confidence—and confidence in them—and may follow your example.

Handling People

Managing your time really comes down to handling people. The reason for clocks, schedules, and calendars relates to dealing with people. A busy administrator fits his appointments and contacts with people into a jigsaw puzzle that, when completed, forms his day.

People are important and you must give your communications with them top priority. One of the best compliments an administrator can be given is that he or she always has time to listen. But what a price an administrator can pay in order to hear that compliment! Often an administrator will sit listening to a staff member while his or her mind is running over a dozen or more things that still need attention.

The administrator should have time for communication with those who need to communicate with him, but he need not give every person an hour of his time. There is an art to bringing a conversation to a close when all that needs to be said has been said. The skillful administrator knows how to close conversations without rushing things.

There are certain techniques that can be used to facilitate conversations. Do not invite a salesman into your office. Instead, meet him at the counter or in the outer office. If his product really interests you, and you want more information, ask him in "for a few minutes." When you have all the information needed, close the conversation by rising, extending your hand, and expressing your gratitude. These are signals that will be read immediately by all but the most insensitive people.

Telephone conversations can be great time-wasters, also. Some people just like to talk and have no idea of your busy schedule. Unless the person is well-known to you, it is good to begin in a businesslike manner. "How can I help you?" will do fine as an opener. It may have to be repeated to keep the caller on the right track. "Thank you for calling; I'll look into the matter" is a good way to close the conversation. If all else fails, try, "May I call you back when I have more time to discuss this?" Whatever technique you use after you have the full message, you must be sensitive to the caller's reading of your attitude.

Some administrators seem to think that giving long periods of time to parents or staff members for aimless conversations will endear them to and give them rapport with those people. More likely the other party will also have time restraints and will wonder how the administrator can spend so much time on such a little matter. The likely conclusion is that the administrator does not have much to do.

People expect an administrator of a modern Christian school to be a busy person with many demands on his time. They expect to state their problem succinctly and to have it considered properly. They do not expect a busy person to waste time in idle conversation. Be kind, courteous, and to the point. End the conversation after an appropriate time and on a positive note. If you follow these suggestions, you will gain respect as an efficient administrator.

This chapter could be extended to include many others facets of time management: ordering supplies (when and how), constructing schedules, delegating tasks, and even filing materials. The administrator is faced with many tasks, large and small. To handle these tasks well, you should become a timesaver, someone who is able to give the ten-minute talk in five minutes. If you are alert and become sensitive to the time robbers, you, too, can become a blue-ribbon timesaver.

9

Developing Empathy

How does one conclude a handbook on Christian-school management? Is some kind of summary, review, or conclusion called for? One need not say anew that which has already been said. On the other hand, it is not appropriate to close this handbook with timesavers. The answer to the questions, "What is this all about? Why was this handbook needed?" comes down to a single word: empathy.

Empathy is the capacity for participating in another's feelings or ideas. The concepts of "empathy" and "Christian," have so much in common that they appear to be mutually inclusive, and one might well consider "Christian empathy" as redundant. Christians worthy of the name have empathy. However, all who have empathy are not by virtue of that empathy Christian.

The Christian-school staff member may have empathy with his or her students. After all, the teacher has been a student, too. The student, on the other hand, is not as likely to have much empathy with a teacher, and surely not with an administrator. That is because the student has not been a teacher or an administrator. The student is likely to have empathy with a fellow student because of shared experiences, and thus can participate in the feelings of fellow students. One tends to have empathy when one has walked in another's shoes.

When we see someone we know go through a sorrow, such as the death of a spouse, we try to empathize with that person. We want to participate in that person's feelings in the hope that our participation will somehow make the loss seem more bearable. We tend to feel a great helplessness because whatever we do or say seems so ineffective.

There is need for empathy in the Christian school, too. There are teachers and administrators who have become lonely in dealing with the problems in the classroom or the school. Teachers sometimes feel the lack of empathy of their students, and sometimes of the students' parents. Sometimes students complain that a certain teacher just doesn't understand. Administrators will say that the burdens of the school have fallen on their shoulders and they really have no one to whom they can turn for advice or help. The administrator is expected to have the answers, not to ask the questions. However, administrators sometimes do not know the answers, and feel that others do not understand because it is impossible to truly empathize with the administrator.

Can you imagine a school where all the students, teachers, board members, and administrators have empathy with each other? Such a school would surely be a Christian school. It would be a school where board members would know when salaries are too low or expectations too high. It would be a school where children would never drive a teacher to tears, depression, or despair. It would be a school where children seldom hear a discouraging word. It would be a school where administrators would not sit in depressed silence looking at the walls after the building or the board room has emptied. It would be a school whose board members would rest well after board meetings. It would be a school where each one involved would realize the special and unique burdens of the other, and would act as if those burdens were his or her own, too.

School management is not only a matter of information, education, and skill. It is a matter of sensitivity, concern, and empathy. That empathy is a gift of God, but not a free gift. It is a gift given only to those who work at and for it.

Your Christian school will have what it needs if those who work in and for it have empathy with each other. Empathy is the key element in Christian-school leadership and management. It is the one essential ingredient which makes a Christian school something very special!